Vegetarians Only

Skybaaba was born in Keshurajupally, near Nalgonda of current Telangana. He later moved to Hyderabad and found work as a journalist, writing for several Telugu dailies, including *Andhra Jyothi*. He is currently a freelance writer and journalist. His published anthologies of poetry include *Jago-Jagao* (2009), *Quit Telangana* (2010) and *Dimmisa* (2011), besides *Zakhmi Awaz* (2012), a collection of his own writings on Telangana. The founder member of Singidi (2010), a Telangana writers' forum, Skybaaba strongly believes there is a need for social movement among Muslims today.

A. Suneetha is Senior Fellow and Coordinator of Anveshi Research Centre for Women's Studies (hereafter Anveshi). A doctorate in political science, her interests include feminist theory and the politics of family, secularism and the Muslim women's question and Muslim politics in Hyderabad. Her articles have appeared in the *Economic and Political Weekly* and the *Indian Journal of Gender Studies*. She is part of the editorial committee of the bilingual quarterly *Anveshi Broadsheet on Contemporary Politics*.

Uma Maheswari Bhrugubanda is Assistant Professor, Department of Cultural Studies, English and Foreign Languages University, Hyderabad, and a member of Anveshi. A doctorate in anthropology from Columbia University, she is currently working on a book on Telugu cinema. Her interests include Telugu literature and cinema, religion and secularism, cinema studies and feminist theory.

Vegetarians Only

Stories of Telugu Muslims

Skybaaba

Translated from the Telugu

Edited by
A. Suneetha
Uma Maheswari Bhrugubanda

Orient BlackSwan

VEGETARIANS ONLY

ORIENT BLACKSWAN PRIVATE LIMITED

Registered Office
3-6-752 Himayatnagar, Hyderabad 500 029, Telangana, India
e-mail: centraloffice@orientblackswan.com

Other Offices
Bengaluru, Bhopal, Chennai, Guwahati, Hyderabad,
Jaipur, Kolkata, Lucknow, Mumbai, New Delhi,
Noida, Patna, Vijayawada

Originally published in Telugu as
Adhure: Muslim Kadhalu (Hyderabad: Nasal Publications, Kitab Ghar, 2012).

First published by Orient Blackswan Private Limited 2016
Reprinted by Orient Blackswan Private Limited 2017

ISBN 978-81-250-6074-1

Illustrations by Akshay Anand Singh of Hyderabad, courtesy of the volume editors.

025571

12052017

Typeset in
Adobe Jenson Pro 11.5/14.2
by Le Studio Graphique, Gurgaon 122 001

Printed in India at
Rakmo Press Pvt. Ltd., New Delhi

Published by
Orient Blackswan Private Limited
3-6-752, Himayatnagar, Hyderabad 500 029, Telangana, India
e-mail: info@orientblackswan.com

Contents

Author's Foreword

My mother had three sisters. My grandmother had five and my father, three. Each of them in turn had daughters. I too have three younger sisters. Almost every one of them is uneducated, socially unaware, and spends her life battling poverty. I have taken part in every celebratory function that occurred in these poor households and helped them out in whatever way I could. I have been part of their highs and lows. It is from being immersed in these lives and relationships that I have emerged as a writer. They are the characters in my stories ... live characters. None of my stories is a work of pure fiction. I have merely narrated things that have happened around me in the form of stories. The troubles of my people have made me restless. Their memories still make me cry. A few stories also emerged from those poor households that I came to know when I used to cycle through the narrow streets of Nalgonda town.

I poured into these stories the misery and penury that mark the lives of Muslims and the consistent betrayal of Muslim political aspirations. The discrimination and oppression that our society subjects Muslims to has greatly pained and disturbed me. My writing is a response to the double standards practiced by society. The eighty-five per cent of non-Muslims in India should understand the truth about the lives of Muslims who live amongst them. They harbour several misconceptions about Muslims, they misunderstand them and suspect them. Hindutva politics makes them do so. But I wanted to demonstrate that what they believe is not true. In reality, most Muslims lead pitiable and miserable lives.

Now that I look back, I feel there are many reasons why I wrote these stories. I was an avid listener of stories since childhood. I would pester my grandmother and grandfather to tell me stories. My father used to read hundreds of Telugu, Hindi and Urdu novels. I would listen keenly when he narrated a few of the good ones to my mother. I would also listen when my mother repeated them to the neighbours. Stories thus became an integral part of my life. This made me read each and every story that I could get hold of. I was also an avid reader of detective novels. I must have read all the detective novels to be found in book-lending shops in Nalgonda town. I was also a regular reader of the children's periodical, *Chandamama,* and of stories and novels published in Telugu weeklies like *Pallaki* or *Swati.*

I love my friends dearly and I am willing to die for them. You can see two of my best friends in these stories. Since I also had the habit of making pen friends, I got used to putting down my thoughts on paper. Whatever length or size the paper was, I made sure that my thoughts would fit into them. Perhaps this habit helped me later on when I switched to writing stories. I developed the craft of narrating stories with brevity.

Many readers told me that these stories opened their eyes to the lives of Muslims. They said that the affection and the relationships in Muslim lives portrayed here were similar to experiences in their own life; that the extreme poverty made them cry. I was surprised to hear from them that the stories helped in dispelling their misconceptions about Muslims and to develop empathy and affection for them. These stories have been more effective than my essays or my speeches. This is precisely why I thought they should reach a wider audience through English translations. I have also been told that such stories of poor Muslims in rural and urban areas in South India are absent in English, which also led me to believe that they should appear in English.

You will notice something special about these stories—they are enveloped in Muslim culture, not Islamic but Indian Muslim culture. You will notice in them themes of Id, wedding, death, phool pehnana, dawat, food culture, dargah culture. The love and affection seen among the poor has entered these stories without my conscious effort. You won't see cars or luxury goods in them. Yet, readers have commented that they have an unputdownable quality about them.

Muslim life has been excluded from the world of Telugu stories. Even Muslims did not write about their own lives. Such a trend truly began with people of my generation with the growth of Muslimvadam. Despite this several writers still hesitate to call their stories Muslim stories. I have put together only those stories that narrate lives of downtrodden Muslims and have confidently called them Muslim stories. Through these stories I want to bring into focus the reality of their lives that remain *adhure,* incomplete or unfinished. This may be one reason why there is much debate on these stories, directly or indirectly.

January 2015 **Skybaaba**

Acknowledgements

First of all, we would like to thank the author Skybaaba for giving us the opportunity to translate his stories. We also thank him for his patience and cooperation during the time it took to complete this work. We thank our co-translators R. Akhileshwari, Christopher Chekuri, D. Vasanta, Kiranmayi Indraganti and Rama Melkote for readily agreeing to translate the stories and for their continued support over the last two years. Our special gratitude to Susie Tharu for her ever-inspiring intellectual camaraderie and warm friendship. Thanks to her also for reading the introduction to this book and giving us valuable feedback.

We wish to thank our colleagues at Anveshi Research Centre for Women's Studies and the Department of Cultural Studies, EFLU, Hyderabad, for creating an atmosphere so conducive to new kinds of intellectual work. We thank Gogu Shyamala and Ashala Srinivas in particular for initiating and enabling a productive collaboration with Skybaaba. The staff at Anveshi has been supportive as always.

We need to thank four people for reading our translations at different stages and encouraging us—Diia Rajan, Deeptha Achar, Pranoo Deshraju and Shahrukh Alam, in particular. Their enthusiasm gave us the necessary courage and conviction to complete the project.

We are thankful to Akshay Anand Singh for the evocative cover image and illustrations done at very short notice.

We are grateful to Veenu Luthria and Roopa Sharma of Orient BlackSwan for their initial interest and continued support for this book. We also thank Moyna Mazumdar for her care and attention to detail and overall help in shepherding this book through its final stages.

And finally we thank our respective families, especially spouses and children, for their love and understanding that make all other efforts worthwhile.

A. Suneetha
Uma Maheswari Bhrugubanda

Of Mofussil Muslim Lives

Her footsteps fell briskly one after another. Her eyes were streaming. Her mind was in turmoil. As she emerged from the by-lane onto the main road, she stubbed her foot against the high edge of the tarred road and stumbled, but she did not fall. There it was, at the far end of the road—the police station! Her heart beat faster. Fear crept through her and she shuddered, her fingers involuntarily clutching at the ends of her burqa. The thought of her son there, inside the police station, brought fresh tears to Mumtaz Begum's eyes and they flowed down her cheeks. Her feet began to move towards the station as if on their own.

–Petition

Osman shut down his shop and started walking home. The lanes were dark. Dogs and pigs were roaming about. Carefully avoiding them, he entered the narrow inner galli, picking his way over the pavement made of cemented shahbad stones. The lane felt congested, just like his mind. On one side there was an open drain reeking of shit; all the houses had open latrines. The pigs mucked around in the drain, grunting, squealing or fighting fiercely.

–Nowhere to Turn

How am I going to manage this wedding, Fatima asked herself for perhaps the hundredth time. Walking briskly against the blazing red sun in a black burqa, she was already drenched in sweat. She had been walking for about fifteen minutes now. By the main road, she would have had to change two autos. One autorickshaw on the straight two-kilometre road, followed by another kilometre to the left in a second autorickshaw. It would probably cost her ten rupees in all—five rupees each way. Instead, if she hit the narrow dust track, it would only be two kilometres across. It would be a half-an-hour walk at most, Fatima told herself, and set off. She was headed to her brother Zameer's place.

–The Benefactor

Some of the most haunting images from Skybaaba's stories are of people walking. Men and women walking in desperation, in anxiety, walking with a faint but undying hope. Many stories open with the protagonist on a quest of some kind—it could be a search for that elusive rented quarter, a search for loans to get a daughter married, a search for the beloved, or a missing son now discovered to be in police custody, or just the walk back home after another miserable day which did nothing to attenuate the stifling oppression of poverty. Many of these quests end in disappointment and despair. But some hold out a glimmer of hope, of unexpected possibilities, of community support even amidst the almost unrelenting sense of helplessness that pervades the world of poor and lower middle-class Telugu Muslims. As Telugu critic K. Srinivas has observed, Skybaaba's stories have most effectively managed to convey the *ekakitanam*, 'the internal and external loneliness' and sense of utter abandonment experienced by the Muslim community (Srinivas 2012).

Vegetarians Only: Stories of Telugu Muslims introduces the English reader, perhaps for the first time, to the life-world of Telugu Muslims, their desires, sorrows, aspirations and predicaments. Skybaaba's stories present touching portraits of Muslim lives battling indigence and prejudice with grace, dignity, love and friendship. Intricate negotiations around dowry and the burqa are interwoven with a communal sharing of marriage expenses and work; the disappointment of unfulfilled love and the grief attending breakdown of marriage are juxtaposed with hope and reconciliation springing from a surprising turn of events; ambivalent promises of migration to the Gulf are thematised even as unfair prejudices and illegal detentions that beset Muslim youth today are subtly but forcefully foregrounded. The stories also depict friendships, camaraderie and sharing between rural and small-town Muslims and Dalits. Written in a simple direct style that details everyday life, going beyond the stereotypes and politicisation of issues, these stories will appeal to a pan-Indian readership.

Shaik Yousuf Baba, who writes under the pen name Skybaaba, is a prolific poet and activist and one of the chief initiators of the literary movement in Telugu called 'Muslimvada Sahityam' which raises pertinent and provocative questions about Muslim identity in contemporary India. In the context of the demolition of the Babri Masjid and the rise of majoritarian Hindutva politics in the 1990s, this movement points to the growing consciousness of 'Muslimness' as an identity upon which to ground a literary as well as a political consciousness. Collections of poems such as *Puttumaccha* (Khader Mohiuddin 1991), *Jihad* (Virasam 1997), *Zalzala* (Skybaaba 1998), *Fatwa* (Khaja 1998) and *Azan* (Anwar and Skybaaba 2002) signalled the birth of this new movement. Apart from the principal concern of countering Hindutva ideology, this literature also gives voice to the question of women's status within Islam and, significantly, caste among Muslims in Andhra Pradesh. Skybaaba has been instrumental in anthologising much of this writing. He has edited three anthologies of Telugu Muslim writings—*Watan: Muslim Kadhalu* (2004)[1], a collection of short stories; *Mulki: Muslim Sahitya Sankalanam* (2005), a collection of poetry, short stories and essays, edited with Vemula Yellaiah; and *Alava: Muslim Sanskruti Kavitvam* (2006), a collection of poetry which he edited with Shajahana. The present volume is a translation of Skybaaba's own first collection of short stories called *Adhure: Muslim Kadhalu* (2012) which raised critical debate in the Telugu literary sphere. Many of these stories were first individually published in different Telugu dailies, periodicals and anthologies such as *Andhra Jyothi, Vaartha, Sakshi, Choopu, Gamanam* (special issue), *Chintha, Navataram Telugu Kadha,* and *Watan.* Skybaaba put them together in *Adhure.*

In his introduction to *Alava*, Skybaaba writes:

> Proper research will prove these facts—In Hyderabad there are Muslim washermen—(dhobis/chakali), barbers—(hajaam/mangali), khasaab (katika), goldsmiths—(sunaar/kansali), carpenters—(badai/vadrangi) and others pursuing such trades. In Nalgonda town, areas like Hyder Khan guda, Manyamchelka, Jam Majeed and Akkachelma are populated by Muslims and dalits in equal numbers. All the houses are mixed up; there is no demarcation between them. This gives us an idea about those who converted to Islam. In all the states in India we find Muslims engaged in a variety of petty trades ... Some reports have stated that Muslims are engaged in more than 60 trades and occupations of the tribals and dalit-bahujans. This makes it evident that it is people from these castes that have converted to Islam.
>
> Before these people converted to Islam they had their caste occupations. But after conversion some of them abandoned their caste professions because they felt that they now belonged to the religion of the nawabs. Yet others abandoned them due to the "low and degrading" status these jobs had in the eyes of brahmin society. Some managed to get clerical and other low level jobs; others acquired agricultural land. However, not being traditional land-owning castes like the reddis, kammas or velamas they were never able to cultivate these lands and in the end, these lands became the property of the reddis, kammas and velamas. The Muslims were soon deprived of both—they had no lands and no occupations. To make matters worse, they had no reservations in education or jobs. So Muslims have been reduced to a truly miserable and pathetic state—they are now literally on the streets. (Shajahana and Skybaaba 2006: 17–18)

In part, it is these observations on the social origins and conditions of the Muslims and their current predicament that shape Skybaaba's understanding of his community and find expression in his fiction as much as they do in his non-fictional work. His own experience of extreme poverty and being a witness to how the destinies of his sisters seemed irrevocably tied to marriage and domesticity, not only lend texture to his accounts of women's oppression but also allow him to evocatively portray their desperate yet courageous struggles. Jani Begum in 'Jani Begum', Fatima Begum in 'The Benefactor' and Mumtaz Begum in 'Petition' are layered portrayals of Muslim women that present their predicaments and their spirited, if unsuccessful, attempts to challenge, negotiate and come to terms with their own lives. The stories are steeped in the Telangana tradition of storytelling—of recounting *vethalu* or sorrows, they are a lament. Well-known political scientist and commentator on Telangana politics K. Srinivasulu has observed that Telangana culture is a culture of sorrow and loss,[2] and the men are not exceptions to this. Skybaaba's male characters are mellow, ordinary non-heroes, struggling against odds, trying to cope with their inability to marry their beloveds, provide for their families, get their sisters married, and find decent employment. The men, as much as the women, freely express their joy and grief, and their vulnerability is palpably present in several stories like 'Nowhere to Turn', 'Sheer Khorma', 'Jani Begum' and 'Urs'.

Some readers might find these stories somewhat didactic, a little too anxious to explain, to plead the cause of the characters as they repeatedly hover around issues such as grinding poverty, the alluring yet uncertain and risky enterprise of finding work and wealth in the Gulf, stifling social customs like early marriage, dowry and the burqa, and the prejudice of caste and community. Certainly, there is a strong desire to record and stand witness to the lives of ordinary Muslims, to record the 'desi Muslim' culture of *urs* and *pirs*, of shared life with Dalits and other lower castes and to give voice to contemporary Muslim concerns. Indeed, it seems that the function of literature here is not simply to give artistic expression to deeply felt emotions or ideas but to perform the role of a witness, to be a vehicle for initiating discussion and debate. In that sense, the stories are an extension of Skybaaba's activism. It is not surprising therefore that the author used *Adhure* as a pretext, as a pamphlet and a testimonial to organise twenty-three meetings around the erstwhile state of Andhra Pradesh, to raise questions and start a discussion about Muslim issues and lives. A second edition of the book, brought out in November 2012 within a year of the first one in 2011, includes an additional forty pages with comments, responses and criticisms of the stories by writers and activists who participated in these meetings. Most of them agree that Skybaaba's stories open a window to marginalised Muslim lives for Telugu readers who have thus far been either ignorant of, or uninterested in, learning about them. They dispel many myths and prejudices to show that ordinary Muslims are just as poor and mired in debt, unemployment and social custom as other castes and communities. Therefore, some have even questioned what is specifically 'Muslim' about these stories. As the Marxist feminist writer Ranganayakamma asks: 'What is there in these stories? a) poverty b) religious conservatism ... Why should they be called Muslim stories? If we replace the Muslim names in these 12 stories with Telugu names, and the burqa with a Telugu conservative practice, won't they become Hindu stories?' (quoted in Skybaaba 2012: 137).

However, it is precisely this sameness *and* difference that marks the Muslim community in Skybaaba's stories. Indeed, for readers of Telugu literature, there may be a familiarity, a sense of déjà vu, especially with stories that thematise marriage, dowry and poverty, for such themes have figured prominently in the work of many writers beginning in the 1940s itself. What is distinctive here is the voice that speaks in these stories and the language it speaks in. While we will have more to say on the question of language later, here we wish to point out that the Muslimness expressed here is not through themes alone (although there are such stories too—'Petition' and 'Homeland' for instance point to specific problems stemming from the minoritisation of Muslims) but also through the setting, characters, and the use of symbols and idioms drawn from the Muslim religious and cultural world. For instance, the moon and moonlight are constant symbols that appear through the stories to connote beauty, prosperity, divine blessings, as also the presence of the beloved and wife. Divinity is experienced through urs and visits to the dargah, which also serve to symbolise the kind of Islam practiced by the protagonists—an accommodative one that shares its culture with non-Muslims. However, the community that the protagonists inhabit is not one that is collectively oriented towards Islamic life or even engaged in fighting for their rights, but something that only materialises at times of need or crisis or even death: to celebrate or mourn—to alleviate their ekakitanam and abandonment by the rest of society, like the extended family in 'Jani Begum', or Saleem in 'The Benefactor'. What also marks Skybaaba's writing is the anxiety and concern around the question of the burqa and its relation to Muslim women's rights. Writing as a Muslim man, he is at pains to re-present the burqa as a symbol of women's subordination as well as denial of freedom within the community. Such an understanding of Muslim women's issues also puts him in the strong Telugu left-liberal tradition that sees all religious customs as irrevocable symbols of unfreedom, especially for women. For instance, Skybaaba presents the character Jani Begum's adoption of the burqa after marriage as the ultimate surrender to patriarchy. We wonder whether there aren't other ways of reading this 'surrender'. The secularism that limits the left-liberal tradition seems to prevent Skybaaba from acknowledging or exploring other ways in which the burqa and other Islamic practices and traditions have been re-imagined and re-adopted by Muslim women in India and across the world. Islam and women's rights are no longer perceived as being antithetical to each other. Initiatives such as preparing a gender-just *nikahnama* and the setting up of women's madrassas in the 1990s in India (Agnes 2012; Suneetha 2012) as well as the worldwide Musawah network (which includes Arab, African, Asian Muslim women and men)[3] are rethinking rights and gender justice from within a reworked Islamic theology.

Skybaaba's stories appear at a crucial historical juncture when hitherto hegemonic Telugu literary, cultural and political identities have begun to unravel. Politically, Telugu identity—which was the basis for the formation of the first linguistic state in India namely,

Andhra Pradesh—does not exist in its old form anymore. The Telangana movement which led to the recent bifurcation of the state into Telangana and Andhra Pradesh is also seen as an opportune time by Skybaaba and other Muslim writers of Telangana to reassert the Deccani culture and the Ganga-Jamuna *tehzeeb* of the region in order to counter narrow political imaginations that try to obscure the intermingling of Hindu and Muslim cultures that mark the long history of the Deccan.

But a good two decades before these political developments, the arrival of feminist, Dalit and minority literatures in the Telugu literary sphere have challenged the predominance of both upper-caste male as well as leftist perspectives. They have introduced new voices, new experiences and new readings that suggest alternate worlds and ethical possibilities. Intermixed with these emerging trends was also another significant move namely, breaking away from the use of standard Telugu. While earlier Telugu fiction featured the use of 'dialect' in dialogue to mark distinctions of class and caste, the narrative voice almost always spoke the standard language. However, these new literatures speak a different Telugu that is marked heavily by its regional, caste and community roots. The authorial voice foregrounds its 'difference' through language itself, not merely through character, setting or theme. Therefore, more and more writers now write in the distinct Telugu dialects of Telangana and Rayalaseema. In the specific case of Muslimvada Sahityam, the regional dialect is further marked by its Urdu lineage. Hence, a mixture of Telugu and Urdu, more specifically Deccani, distinguishes the language of many Muslim writers writing in Telugu.

There is a complex history of the language issue that is only now beginning to be acknowledged with the formation of Telangana. When Andhra Pradesh was formed as a linguistic state, the adoption of Telugu identity and the educational and language policies that followed from it led to the devaluing of schooling in Urdu as also to its narrow identification with the Muslim community. So, ironically while being learned in the former Hyderabad state meant being fluent in Urdu, in Andhra Pradesh learning Urdu came to be regarded as a conservative and backward move. Therefore, Muslims like Skybaaba, who spoke Deccani at home but who were part of the public education system, never learnt to read and write Urdu but did all their schooling in Telugu and became part of the Telugu literary public sphere. There are also many Muslims who studied in Urdu medium schools and madrassas and who are active in the Urdu literary and political spheres. The linguistic chasm that divides these Muslims who live in the same state has meant that intellectual traffic between these two worlds has been very limited, if not non-existent and hence, Muslim discourse has followed very different trajectories in the two languages.

In his foreword to the Telugu edition of these stories, writer and scholar Mohammed Afsar names the language used by Skybaaba 'Telugurdu'. As Skybaaba himself notes, most Muslims in Telangana speak Deccani at home, Telangana Telugu mixed liberally with Urdu words in the social sphere, and use standard Telugu in public writing and writing for the media. In that sense, these stories are already translations of a certain kind. Skybaaba translates the Deccani Muslim world into Telugu for his Telugu readers. This translatedness is evident in many stories where in the course of a narrative, a Deccani word is translated into Telugu and given in brackets. For instance, *sheer khorma* transcribed in Telugu is followed by *payasam* in brackets. Terms like *lein-dein, maseri palang,* and *dastar* are also followed by their Telugu equivalents. Many cultural and social rituals are described and explained at length because the assumed reader of these stories is believed (and rightly so) to be by and large ignorant of these practices. The lengthy description of the *gulposhi* or sending-off ceremony in 'Nowhere to Turn' when Osman is set to leave for Saudi and the funeral ceremonies in 'Life in Death' are two striking examples. Our own translations are, in that sense, paradoxical, as they may read and sound like translations of translations. Skybaaba's Telugurdu, while being the most interesting and distinctive feature of these stories, also poses the greatest challenge for translation. We have retained some Telugu and several Urdu words in the English translations to give readers a feel of this language and some of its texture, but we know we have only been partially successful in this attempt.

Nevertheless, what we want to foreground through these translations is the fact that Skybaaba and other Muslim writers writing in Telugu challenge and trouble sedimented categories such as 'Telugu' and 'Muslim'. Confronted with the demands of the newly assertive marginalised vernaculars, the regional and linguistic identity of Telugu had to lose some of its rigidity to make way for new questions, new identities and a newly configured readership comprising Telugu Muslims. Telugu and Muslim have often been thought of as distinct and separate (as evident from Ranganayakamma's comment cited above). By bringing the two together, another identity too is questioned—that of the Indian Muslim. Commonsensical thinking lumps together Muslims across language, caste, region and class without attempting a dialogue or democratic consensus among them. The Telugurdu of Skybaaba's stories brings into focus the diverse and chequered histories of diverse Muslim communities in different parts of the country and across different castes.

Our attempt has been to introduce the English-speaking world to a significant contemporary Telugu writer whose stories illuminate the everyday lives of poor Telugu Muslims with insight and empathy. The context of their production also provides a rare glimpse into the difficulty and complexity of forging public cultures in a turbulent time of political reconfigurations such that minority cultures are not merely tolerated but duly acknowledged and accommodated.

August 2015

A. Suneetha
Uma Maheswari Bhrugubanda

NOTES

1. This is a collection of 52 stories by 39 Muslim writers. The writers Smail and Dadahayath were guest editors; Khaja, Shajahana, Inayatullah, Abbaas and Gaus Mohiuddin were part of the editorial board.

2. 'In contrast, the strength of the Telangana movement is drawn from the cultural sphere. It has given rise to an upsurge of cultural production in the form of song-performance and of course fiction. In these resurgent folk cultural forms of expression, Telangana is configured as both worthy of celebration and also mourning. The dialectic of mourning and celebration, sense of loss and presence and despair and hope in interesting ways contrast Telangana with coastal Andhra.' (Srinivasulu 2011)

3. For details see http://www.musawah.org/about-musawah

REFERENCES

Agnes, Flavia. 2012. 'Economic Rights of Women in Islamic Law'. *Economic and Political Weekly* 31(41–42): 2832–38.

Anwar, and Skybaaba, eds. 2002. *Azan: Gujarat-Muslim Kavitvam.* Hyderabad: Dardi Publications.

Khaja. 1998. *Fatwa*. Palvoncha: Kala Publications.

Ranganayakamma. 2012. In *Adhure: Muslim Kadhalu,* Skybaaba. Haryali Muslim Rachayitala Vedika. 137. Hyderabad: Nasal Publications, Kitab Ghar.

Shajahana, and Skybaaba eds. 2006. *Alava: Muslim Sanskruti Kavitvam*. Nalgonda: Nasal Publications, Kitab Ghar.

Skybaaba. 2012. *Adhure: Muslim Kadhalu*. Haryali Muslim Rachayitala Vedika. Hyderabad: Nasal Publications, Kitab Ghar.

——, ed. 1998. *Zalzala: Muslimvada Kavitvam*. Nalgonda: Nilagiri Sahiti.

——, ed. 2004. *Watan: Muslim Kadhalu*. Nalgonda: Nasal Publications, Kitab Ghar.

——, and Vemula Yellaiah, eds. 2005. *Mulki: Muslim Sahitya Sankalanam*. Hyderabad: Hyderabad Book Trust.

Srinivas, K. 2012. 'Charita oka Bhaaram, Vartamanam oka Gaayam' (The Past is a Burden, the Present, a Wound). In *Adhure: Muslim Kadhalu*, Skybaaba. 18. Haryali Muslim Rachayitala Vedika. Hyderabad: Nasal Publications, Kitab Ghar.

Srinivasulu, K. 2011. 'The Bluff of Samaikyandhra'. In *Interrogating Reorganization of States: Culture, Identity and Politics in India*, eds. Asha Sarangi and Sudha Pai. 4. New Delhi: Routledge.

Suneetha, A. 2012. 'Muslim Women and Marriage Laws: Debating the Model Nikahnama'. *Economic and Political Weekly* 42(43): 40–48.

1
Jani Begum

'Bhai, does anyone ask Lattibbi who works as a daily wage labourer to wear a burqa? Or demand that Shabana Azmi, Benazir Bhutto or even Shamina Khala, who moves around in a car to be in purdah? Why is all the attention focused on women like me?'

Jani Begum's question stopped me in my tracks. I had just returned from Nalgonda town. I changed into a lungi and re-entered the house after having a wash in the backyard. My sister followed me out to the backyard and back into the house, recounting all that our khalba had accused her of that morning. Struggling for an appropriate response to her earlier query which was still buzzing in my head, I kept listening. I could not help saying, 'It is none of his business. You should have told him that we know our customs quite well and ... anyway times have changed'. Encouraged by my response, she enthusiastically recounted her argument with khalba.

Jani Begum, my younger sister, never said yes to what she disliked. Nor did she ever adjust or compromise on any matter. This made her quite unpopular among our relatives who never lost an opportunity to point a finger at her. It disturbed my parents no end. They pestered her to be more like a girl and to wear a burqa when she went out. But chelle would not heed. Over time, they stopped saying such things. Meanwhile, she entered her second year of the Intermediate.

Occasionally, quarrels would break out between ammi and Jani Begum. Once, I had just returned from Nalgonda. As I entered the house, I heard ammi scolding her in a loud voice. Chelle did not keep quiet. Her insolent responses angered ammi even more and her voice reached a higher pitch. I found both of them in the front yard. Ammi was picking grit from the rice while chelle sat on a small stool in front of her with a book in her hand.

'What happened? Why are you both quarrelling?'

'Just look at her! I had gone to Nalgonda haat, expecting that she would at least cook the rice by the time I returned. But she did nothing of the sort. How can I do all the house work by myself! And all she says is: I have to study! Let me see what she does next year. I swear I will make sure that she stays at home! She won't be able to shirk all this work then.'

'No, you cannot do that! I won't keep quiet,' Jani Begum shot back. 'Come what may, I won't stop studying until *I* want to!'

Before mother could respond, I intervened, 'Please stop this now. You two are forever arguing over petty things'. I pulled chelle inside, pleading, 'Why can't you keep quiet for once? When you know ammi is angry, why do you persist in annoying her even more!'

As my sister grew older, such quarrels between them became more frequent. 'Stubborn wretch! Always does what she wants. What use is all my shouting and nagging!' mother would complain. My younger brother also strongly disapproved of her ways, so she could not get along with him either. In poor Muslim families like ours, fathers are the biggest villains as far as daughters are concerned. The brothers, older and younger come next. The rest of the extended family does not lag far behind in prescribing dos and don'ts.

As soon as she cleared her tenth standard exams, ammi, abba and all our close relatives declared, 'She need not study any further. Let's get her married this year.' But chelle said, 'No. I want to go to college.'

I was her lone supporter. I had a hard time arguing her case with ammi and abba. 'There are so few educated girls amongst us. It is hard to find someone who has cleared her tenth exams. Jani Begum is an intelligent girl. Let us not think like everyone else and force her to quit now.' After much persuasion, they finally agreed. I sighed with relief. Chelle was delighted. But ammi persisted, 'What if we find a nice groom while she is still in college?' In that case, I said, we could put a stop to her education. Satisfied with this response, ammi was quiet.

Jani Begum cleared all her exams both in the first and second years. She did not fail in a single subject. I was overjoyed. But trouble began soon after that. I wanted to enrol her in a B.A. programme. The family did not agree. 'Where will you get the money from?' they asked. 'Will *you* get her married? If we get her married now, our close relatives are ready to help. We cannot afford to postpone it any longer.' Of course, they were also indirectly rebuking me for my joblessness. I felt helpless. As the last date for submitting the application approached, chelle grew increasingly distressed. I, too, was upset and anxious. I couldn't bear to see her sitting at home. Not knowing what to say, I would keep avoiding her. I would escape to nearby Nalgonda, spend the whole day there and return late in the evening only after everyone had gone to bed. Those were really difficult days.

I realised that there were several issues behind keeping Jani Begum away from college. The college was far from home, nearly six kilometres away. The very thought of a grown up girl going there all alone made the family jittery. And her refusal to wear a burqa made matters worse. As if this were not enough, my uncle once spotted her talking to a boy. Someone even saw her in a cinema theatre with her girl friends. I would get really annoyed when these complaints reached me, especially when they went on about it as if they were great transgressions. I would generally let them pass without comment. Occasionally, I would react sharply, 'So what? What's wrong in going to the cinema? Should girls be jailed at home? Times have changed. You can't expect her to live the way you did!' They would turn against me, 'You are spoiling the girl. Anyway, it is up to you. Do what you like.'

Despite all this, I continued to support Jani Begum until she completed her Intermediate. Emboldened by this, she continued going on excursions sponsored by the college, or for tutorials, or to visit close relatives and friends, and do whatever else she wanted. I was given the task of convincing my parents whenever she wanted to do any of these things. She even managed to attend her friends' weddings.

But she steadfastly and persistently refused to cook. Washing utensils and fetching water from the street tap were the only household duties that she willingly took on. For anything else, she would declare with characteristic stubbornness, 'I have to study.'

Ammi tried hard to convince her, 'How will you cook at your in-laws' if you don't learn now?'

Chelle replied, 'There is no need for it now. I can learn after I'm married.'

'If you don't cook well, your husband will thrash you and throw you out of the house!'

'As if I would stand for such nonsense!' she retorted. 'I will thrash him in return and leave him!'

No one could resist a giggle at this.

When she wasn't allowed to join the B.A. course, Jani Begum grew even more recalcitrant. She would only do the chores that she chose to, and turn a deaf ear to what everyone had to say. She would answer them with her silence. But she still continued to do what she liked, whether it was visiting her aunt's house or going to the cinema.

My parents began to search for a groom for Jani Begum. Initially they looked for a man with a sarkari job. Having witnessed the difficulties faced by my elder sister with a husband in a private job, they were keen to send the younger one to a household that was better off. Half a dozen young men with government jobs came to see her, but they all left in no time. On each of these occasions, the household would go topsy-turvy. Chelle would be decked up like a bride and shown to the prospective groom's family. The dahej discussion would follow, with the groom's family quoting the amount. As soon as my parents disclosed the dowry we could afford, the marriage talks would inevitably fall through. After going through several such exercises, my parents realised that a salaried damad was out of reach for them. They began to look for a self-employed groom. Half a dozen self-employed grooms visited our house, but none of these visits materialised in marriage. Two years passed by in these efforts. The failure to find a suitable groom and the ensuing questions and taunts from close relatives perturbed my parents. Even my uncles and aunts began to feel the heat.

During these two years, I was a witness to the intense internal conflict that Jani Begum went through. Wilful and naughty by nature, she was always demanding things from my parents or quarrelling with her younger brother. But now, she put an end to all that. Ammi was saddened to find that the frequent and fierce verbal duels with her ceased completely. Chelle's willingness to compromise was depressing. Initially she had demanded an employed groom even if it meant taking a loan on the house. Now she was willing to get married to anyone. Her entire bearing changed. Her face wore a desolate look and she appeared withdrawn.

Sometimes I wished we would sell the house and other valuables to get her married with sufficient dowry. I even hoped that she would fight for it. But though she never uttered a word, Jani Begum seemed to have understood the situation and resigned herself to it. I wondered if things would have come to such a pass if she had continued her studies. Would they have?

Meanwhile, a suitable alliance was found by my aunt's family. The groom was a driver. We had to agree to a higher amount towards the jode ki rakham and lein-dein than we were prepared for. Jani Begum was engaged in ten days' time and the wedding was scheduled to take place in a month and a half.

Once the wedding date was fixed, the household went into frenzied preparations. Thanks to all the hectic activity, most of us even lost some weight. But ammi took the brunt of it. Her feet would get swollen with all the running around, especially in mobilising support from her brothers, sisters and other relatives. As abba had no head for such matters, ammi had to take them on. Once that was done, she went on a shopping expedition with her sister to Charminar in Hyderabad where everything—from combs to clothes—was cheaper. I took care of the remaining sundry tasks.

My maternal uncle, ammi's younger brother gave ten thousand rupees towards the jode ki rakham. Each of the paternal uncles gave a tola of gold. One of ammi's sisters gave a steel cupboard, and the other, the maseri palang. Grandmother gave some money and each of my older sisters gave a thousand rupees each. Other close relatives gave a fan or a clock and so on. In our community, this is a regular practice—of relatives contributing to the wedding expenses in a poorer household in cash or in kind. In turn, we would support weddings in their households.

On the day of the wedding, there was a festive atmosphere all around. Relatives arrived early and filled all the rooms. The ones occupied by women relatives looked most colourful, as if the choicest blossoms had been put together. It was a visual feast with everyone wearing new clothes freshly taken out of shopping bags. The house had just got a new roof made for the wedding. Outside, both the tents were filled with people clad in the latest styles of kurta-pyjama and caps. The whole place looked like a garden swaying in the breeze. My maternal and paternal uncles were busy cooking in the tent behind the house.

We, the immediate family, were oblivious to all this festivity and enthusiasm of the relatives. We were so busy making sure that everyone was comfortable and taken care of that we had not even bothered to wear new clothes or beautify ourselves. We were much too anxious about the arrival of the wedding party, the groom's side. If we failed to make proper arrangements for their comfort or if anything went wrong, it would surely result in a scene. Everything must be done on time. Every last little detail must be attended to. The groom must be supplied with hot water for his bath. Once he is dressed, the bride's family must welcome him in the appropriate manner. A tent had been put up in front of our house and a mattress, meant for the maseri palang, was arranged to seat the groom and the qazi who would read the nikah. Women of the household were busy preparing the bride. It was as if we were preparing for battle.

The nikah was read, and the dawat was soon over. The guests took a break to rest for a while. In the evening, once the jalwa was completed, the groom's family wanted to head back to their village. From the inner rooms, Jani Begum's loud wails could be heard. I was restlessly pacing the yard. After a while I could bear it no longer and walked into her room. She looked up as I entered. I sat down next to her, drew her close to me and we wept. She was sobbing aloud, calling out, 'Bhaiya, bhaiya' in between sobs. Our tearful embrace made everyone else around—my parents, other siblings, uncles and aunts—tearful. A distant relative tried to separate us, declaring that I needed to control my emotions. 'My boy, you shouldn't cry like this! You will break your sister's heart!' But I shook her off. Others also tried to console us, but in vain. Neither of us could contain our emotions.

Hearing the wails and the commotion, my maternal uncle came into the house and said, 'Beta, you should not cry like a woman. Come now, get up and get going. There is a lot of work to do. Her luggage has to be loaded onto the bus. Come on, let us go now'. And he almost dragged me out of there.

As we loaded her luggage onto the bus, Jani Begum took her leave, tearfully embracing every family member and friend in turn. The sun had set and the lights were turned on. But for my family it was as if their life was being drained out of their limbs. They slowly led my sister to the bus. Abba, who had kept his distance from all this till now, could no longer hold back his emotions as she drew closer. Chelle put her arms around him and sobbed like a child. Until then, I had never seen abba cry.

Someone from the groom's side came up and said, 'Hurry up, we are getting late'.

Father and daughter were separated and she was led forward. By now, everyone, including children, neighbours and some villagers were looking on with moist eyes. Such a long bout of weeping had exhausted ammi. Her eyes had sunk into their sockets and her face grown dark with sorrow. Supported by an aunt, she walked with difficulty, holding the edge of her saree over her mouth.

At last the bus departed, slowly and reluctantly, manoeuvring with difficulty through the endless consolations, cautions, counsels, reassurances and farewells.

It was impossible to sleep that night. I slept in the yard on two bare tables joined at the edges. The tables had been hired for the wedding. I had no blanket to cover myself or a sheet to cover the tables. I tossed and turned, but I could not erase the image of a sobbing Jani Begum from my mind. I could not stop thinking, my little chelle is gone ... the one I had carried on my shoulders, the one who always supported my words and deeds, the one who made the household lively. The house will turn silent now. How will she cope with her new family? Will my brother-in-law take proper care of her? He seems to be a good man, but what kind of a person is he really? Will she like him? It is a pity they did not even get a glimpse of each other before the wedding. Sigh! I tossed on those hard tables. Everyone was asleep from exhaustion. Then, I saw father quietly get up in the dark and light a cigarette. There was an eerie silence, broken only by my mother's muffled sobs.

The walima was to be held the next day at the groom's house. They were informed that fifty of us would attend. To reach their village, we would take the afternoon bus from ours. By the time the bus reached their village, it would be evening.

The next morning we ate bagara rice with lentils, left over from last night's dinner. Then we got busy cleaning the huge pile of vessels and dismantling the tents as everything needed to be returned to the tent-house. In the meantime, the relatives started playing chouthi. In no time, the front yard became messy with people trying to spray water or rub soot on each other's faces or throw each other into the mud. I was standing on one side and counting the rented folding chairs when my brother-in-law came running out of nowhere, lifted me bodily in his arms and dumped me into a tub of water! My younger brother rushed to rub soot onto my brother-in-law's face. My mother and her sisters-in-law were playing in another corner. My maternal uncles had put so much colour on my father that he could not be recognised. In turn, abbu joined his brothers-in-law in chasing my other mamus. The front yard turned boisterous with shrieks, laughter and jokes till noon.

I could not attend the walima due to all the pending chores. My friends were very reluctant to go without me, but I insisted. They got irritated with me, but went ahead anyway. It was midnight by the time they all returned to our village in the tractor. Jani Begum and bhai jaan, however, were not with them. Apparently their family had decided that the newlywed couple would visit my family only after the first jummagi. Many relatives reported to me that chelle had inquired after me, and when she realised I hadn't come, she had wept. I felt miserable.

I spent the next six days waiting for Jumma, thinking of her every second. Finally, the day arrived. I got ready early to take the first bus to their village. There were only two buses to their village, one in the morning and another in the afternoon. I took the early morning bus. Alighting in their village, I asked around for directions to their house, mentioning the names of my brother-in-law and his father. After roaming up and down a few streets, I found their house at last.

The door was ajar. Inside, there was a big yard. As soon as I entered the house, the first person I saw was Jani Begum. Squatting next to the water tap on the left, she was washing a huge pile of dirty dishes. Back home, I had never seen her wash so many vessels at one go. I was shocked that she was given such a lot of work so soon after the wedding. I stood there, stunned.

At the sound of the door, she turned to see who it was, and she got up and ran towards me without even wiping her hands clean. 'Salam alaikum, bhaiya!' she greeted me joyfully. Patting her head, I asked how she was. Her eyes turned moist with emotion.

'Where is bhai jaan?' I inquired of her husband.

'He went into the village to meet someone', she replied.

Her mother-in-law emerged from the inner quarters. I paid her my respects. Chelle went to the verandah to get a charpai for me to sit on. I sat there, exchanging pleasantries with phuppamma. Soon, her father-in-law and sisters-in-law also came out along with some other relatives. I paid them my respects and answered all their queries with a smile. Jani Begum stood by my side in silence. After a while, phuppa suggested that I have a wash. Chelle went inside and brought a soap and towel for me. I washed myself near the tap. She went in again to get water for me to drink. Phuppamma called me inside. I followed her without quite knowing why. Once I crossed that room, I found myself in an enchanted space. There was a washroom on one side and a woodstove on the other. The washroom had a jasmine bush growing thickly over it for a roof, and its shadow fell on the floor. The roof above the woodstove slanted onto the adjacent street, leaving a triangular window in between.

The light from the window lit up the whole place. Somehow I liked that place immensely.

A mat was spread on the floor near the woodstove. There was toddy in a big pot. An empty pot sat next to it. It was then that I realised what they were doing inside until then. I was asked to sit down. Phuppamma gave me a bowl of boiled horsegram, hot and fresh from the vessel on the woodstove. Phuppa served me toddy in a steel glass. It was good. I drank another glass but declined when I was offered a third. But I took another helping of the horsegram. Sprinkled with salt and chilli powder, it was delicious.

We sat there chatting as we ate and drank. Chelle joined us. 'Bhai, how is ammi?' she asked. I told her ammi was fine. Despite my insistence, she refused to sit next to me. But when phuppamma told her to, she obliged. Phuppa gave her a glass of toddy. She took two sips with some reluctance, and got up. I sat there for a long time and drank four more glasses of toddy. Then I was served khichdi-khatta, the staple food of Jumma, with papad and finished the meal with kheer. I took a nap on the cot in the yard.

When I woke up, it was evening and my brother-in-law had returned. He took me into the village to meet his friends. They were all farmers who had discontinued their studies to take up farming. We went to a goundla house for toddy. My brother-in-law bought a pot of twelve litres. In the course of the conversation, I realised that one of his friends was a shudra and the other, a madiga. The goundla man served them in cups made of moduga leaves, and us in glasses. I felt that I was being respected because I was educated and light-skinned. I didn't drink much as I was not in the habit of drinking toddy. But they all took another pot of four litres.

It was already dark by the time we returned home. Jani Begum was waiting for us. A dinner of country chicken was served. My bed was made in the verandah as I wanted to sleep there. The rest of them—all our in-laws, their relatives, children, and that beautiful girl who caused a flutter in my heart—slept in the courtyard.

Chelle brought me a tumbler of water, kept it under the cot and told me to call her if I needed anything. We chatted briefly before she went inside, but I knew that she would be thinking of me. She was aware that this was my first overnight visit to any relative's place. One half of my cot was in the shade of the verandah and the other stretched out. Lying on the cot, I felt as if even the sky and the stars somehow seemed different and new. Neem trees on the street were humming in the night breeze. I went to sleep, lulled by the village breeze and the toddy.

When I woke up, chelle was sweeping the big yard outside the house. Then she swept the empty yard inside. I went out to look for a neem stick for brushing my teeth. Father-in-law, who was returning from the village tank, extended his hand towards me, holding out two sticks. I took the thicker one.

We washed up and had rice for breakfast. Chelle finished her chores and got ready to leave. I could hear her hurrying up her husband. She brought out her suitcase and a bag and kept them in the verandah. Bhai jaan came out, wearing a new shirt and trousers. I took the suitcase in my hand. Chelle looked pretty in a new saree. She took something from the bag her husband was carrying and went inside. I took leave from her in-laws. They wanted to accompany us to the bus stand. I also bid farewell to their other relatives. The eyes of that beautiful girl and her smile remained imprinted on my heart.

My brother-in-law called out, 'Jani Begum, it is getting late, hurry up! If we miss this bus, we will have to wait until four in the afternoon.' That worried me. Annoyed, I turned back to see what was taking her so long. Just then chelle came out. I couldn't believe my eyes. Jani Begum was standing there in full burqa. For ten long years, hadn't she been endlessly scolded and rebuked and censured just because she had steadfastly refused to wear one? My eyes were welling up, my mind was clouding over with conflicting emotions. She must have sensed what I was going through, and my reflection in her eyes streamed down her cheeks along with her tears.

Translated by **A. Suneetha**

2

Petition

Her footsteps fell briskly one after another. Her eyes were streaming. Her mind was in turmoil. As she emerged from the by-lane onto the main road, she stubbed her foot against the high edge of the tarred road and stumbled, but she did not fall. There it was, at the far end of the road—the police station! Her heart beat faster. Fear crept through her and she shuddered, her fingers involuntarily clutching at the ends of her burqa. The thought of her son there, inside the police station, brought fresh tears to Mumtaz Begum's eyes and they flowed down her cheeks. Her feet began to move towards the station as if on their own.

At the station gates, she paused, unsure if she should enter. After a moment's hesitation, Mumtaz Begum walked in. Keeping to the side of the path, she approached the policeman on guard.

'What do you want?' he asked her gruffly.

'Listen, beta! My son is inside. I am really anxious to see him. Can you please tell him this?'

'What did he do? What case has he been booked under?'

'I don't know! There is no case, nothing. They just brought him away for nothing at all. It's been fifteen days now. Beta, believe me, my son is a very good lad. He hasn't harmed anyone. He hasn't done anything wrong—I know him very well.'

'My superior is not here. Go away! Come back tomorrow.'

'No beta. I will wait here until he comes back. I cannot live without seeing my son. Please help me!'

'All right. You can wait there until the big officer arrives', the policeman said, displaying some sympathy at last.

Mumtaz Begum slowly climbed up the steps and sat down on a bench that stood on one side. She wiped her tears and blew her nose.

'When will the Saab arrive, son?'

'I don't know', said the policeman, a little irritated.

Mumtaz Begum found herself bursting into tears at the slightest pretext. The thought that her son was right here in this station, in one of the rooms inside, made her cry even more.

She would become restless if she didn't see him even for a couple of days. He, too, would never stay away for more than a day or two, even when he needed to travel out of town. And they brought him here so unfairly! Now they were refusing to let him go! Soon after the arrest, Pasha Miyan had roamed around for nearly four days, meeting a lot of people in the hope of getting his son out. A couple of small-time political leaders had also accompanied him to the police station and spoken to the Sub-Inspector. The SI had angrily retorted, 'Don't we know what to do! Should you be coming to tell us?!' He was a real crook who refused to listen to anyone. Pasha Miyan had even approached the local MLA. But the MLA said, 'SI Ravikanth Reddy is not a good man, not someone we can negotiate with. He doesn't care for anyone. I will go there only to return empty-handed. It is better if you go talk to him'. Pasha Miyan had next gone to a Communist Party leader. But even he had a similar tale to tell. He had gone to meet Ravikanth Reddy just the day before in connection with another boy's arrest. 'This man has linked these boys to all kinds of things and framed them in serious cases. I don't think there is much that we can do now', the leader had concluded. After this, Pasha Miyan had given up completely and refused to budge out of the house.

Mumtaz Begum sat there for a long time, thinking, wiping her tears, blowing her nose. In between she asked the policeman on guard twice, 'Beta, has the SI come in?'

'I don't know, ma. He may come, he may not come.'

At last, when it began to get dark, she got up. 'Tell me what should I do, son?' she asked.

'Come back early tomorrow, ma. SI Sir will be there.'

Mumtaz Begum got up with effort, though her limbs refused to move. She looked hopefully at the policeman and again pleaded, 'Won't you please just let my son know that I am here?'

'No, ma. Not possible. We can see him only with SI Sir's permission.'

She did not want to leave. She walked a few slow steps, then turned around to look at the station. Her son was still there, trapped within those four walls.

'Go. Go away. Don't stand here crying. Go!' said another policeman stepping out from inside the gates.

Mumtaz Begum moved away. She began to curse loudly even as she wept. She cursed the policemen and her own community's wretched helplessness.

A crow cawed loudly as it flew around in circles, frantically looking for her little one that had fallen out from the nest.

The following morning, Mumtaz Begum was back at the station by ten o'clock. There seemed to be a lot of hectic activity inside. The policeman on duty at the gate did not let her enter. She stood at some distance, looking on. Her son was inside. But they won't let her see him. She had long dreamt of a son. She had borne him with great care. She had given him birth at great risk to her own life. She and her husband had nurtured their son with love, going hungry themselves. He was more precious to them than life itself. And then the police had come for him like thieves in the middle of the night. Her son, who had never known beatings of any kind, was thrashed with a baton. He was kicked around with those heavy boots and dragged away. Their repeated anxious queries and fervent appeals make no difference to the police. They do not respond. They do not care. How can they accuse and punish an entire neighbourhood claiming that some Muslims had done something somewhere?! Mumtaz Begum walked purposefully towards the station.

The policeman stopped her outside the gate. 'Listen beta, I came yesterday and they asked me to come back today. My son is inside. I want to see him just once.'

'Can't you understand! You cannot go in today! Some big officers will be visiting. They won't let anyone in today. Go away!'

Mumtaz Begum tried to say something but the policeman shouted at her again. She went back to where she was standing before. She waited a long while. Then she headed back home.

'Sir ... Sir, this woman, Buamma has been sitting here for a long time, Sir. She has been coming here every day for the past four days. She says Ahmad is her son. Please Sir, she wants to see him just once, Sir', pleaded Constable Janaiah.

SI Ravikanth Reddy was walking down the steps leading out of the station when he heard this. 'Ask her to come after two days,' he said, getting into his jeep. The jeep sped away.

Janaiah turned towards Mumtaz Begum with a heavy heart. He knew well how helpless people like him felt when confronted by the likes of Ravikanth Reddy who enjoyed both the power of law and the authority of caste. Mumtaz Begum just stood there and stared with sunken eyes and a lifeless gaze. Her slippers on the verge of breaking, her feet badly cracked, her legs frail and tired, she stood there in a faded burqa and stared, wringing her hands, twisting and untwisting her long bony fingers.

The crow continued its frantic circling.

'Oh! You should have come a little earlier, Buamma. The SI just left,' said Janaiah.

'Beta, since you said I could meet Ahmad today, I made his favourite cucumber dal and fried kebabs. I got a little late by the time I got the tiffin carrier ready,' Mumtaz Begum reported anxiously.

Constable Janaiah was moved by the plight of this mother making daily trips to the station in the hope of seeing her son. Day before, he had again asked Ravikanth Reddy if she could see her son. Reddy had left without a word. Janaiah didn't know what to say. 'Come again tomorrow, Buamma. I am sure they will tell you something tomorrow,' he had said to console her. She had left overjoyed by this news. And today, she had come after the SI had left. What was the use! Janaiah wondered what to say to her now.

Mumtaz Begum just stood there without moving. He asked her, 'Don't you have anyone else, Buamma? It would be good if someone else also came along with you, asking for Ahmad. The SI is so callous because you have been coming here alone looking for the boy.'

Mumtaz Begum stood staring at the tiffin carrier in her hands. She looked up and asked, 'Beta, have they been giving food to my son? He cannot stay hungry for long. He has to eat something as soon as it is meal time, even if it is just pickle and rice. How is my Ahmad? Why won't you let me see him just once?' Grief choked her words, she was finding it difficult to speak.

Janaiah didn't know how to respond. He was moved to tears listening to her. 'When there was so much trouble all around, why didn't you send your son out of town for a few days? Look, now they are thrashing him so badly!'

'What! What did you say? ... They are beating my ... my son!'

Janaiah was shaken. He quickly collected himself and said, 'No, no, Buamma, they are not beating him! Just questioning him.'

'What are they questioning him about? What are they asking him?'

'Well ... they want to know if he is involved ... If he is in any way connected to all the disturbances.'

'But what has he got to do with all the trouble?!' Mumtaz Begum's voice was breaking. 'He hardly goes out of the house. After completing his studies here in Nalgonda, he wanted to go to Hyderabad. But we couldn't afford it. Perhaps we should have sent him away ... Since then he had been at home, giving tuitions. His father sells bananas. What he earns is hardly enough to run the house. We have another daughter waiting to be married off ...' Mumtaz Begum's voice trailed off.

'Buamma, come back early tomorrow, meet the SI, and speak to him personally. He might listen to you.'

'But they had picked up another boy called Ramesh along with my son. Today, I saw him at a distance, trying to avoid me. So how is that they have released him but won't let my son go?'

'Ayyo! It is not just your son, ma! There are ten other Muslim boys who have also been picked up. No one cares about them. There were two of them who were able to use money or influence—they managed to get out. There are a couple of others like you who have been running around the station for days. Some are even afraid to come here. The SI here is known to be a cruel chap. He doesn't listen to anyone. He is particularly reluctant to let go of any Muslims he gets hold of. I will try talking to the Assistant SI. Come again tomorrow, Buamma.'

'Sir, it is Ahmad's mother, Sir. She is coming here every day, Sir. Sir, she just wants to see Ahmad once,' the Assistant SI was saying to the SI. Sub-Inspector Ravikanth Reddy, who was striding down the verandah, stopped and turned to look at Mumtaz Begum. She took a few hesitant steps towards him and said, 'Sir, my Ahmad is innocent. He is my only son. Our house is so gloomy without him. None of us has been able to eat or drink properly. His sister hasn't eaten at all for days now. Please let him go,' she pleaded. Then Mumtaz Begum wiped her tears, looked up at the Sub-Inspector and said, 'At least let me see him once. I and everyone at home will feel reassured. Please Sir! I beg of you, let me see him once!'

Reddy turned towards the ASI and said in English, 'He's not in a state to move at all. Letting her see him now would mean that word will get around, and there will be a big row. Ask her to come after a few days.' Saying this, Ravikanth Reddy went inside.

Mumtaz Begum didn't understand a word of what he said. She was looking anxiously at the Assistant Sub-Inspector. The ASI looked at Constable Janaiah and told him in English that he should speak to the woman and somehow send her away for now. And he too disappeared inside.

Janaiah walked up to her and said, 'Buamma, it is not possible to see him now. They are asking you to come after four days.'

'Why? Son, why?! Why won't you show my Ahmad to me? You have been making me run around this place for so many days! What has he done? Why won't you let him go? You won't even let me see him once at the very least! I am not going to keep quiet anymore. You think there is no one to question you, don't you?!' Mumtaz Begum raised her voice and started shouting at them.

The Sub-Inspector said something sharply from inside. Two policemen marched out of the room clicking their boots and gruffly ordered her, 'Look woman, no shouting here. We don't want to hear another word from you. Now just go away!'

Mumtaz Begum, who had never cursed anyone in her life because she didn't know how to curse properly, heaped curses on those policemen in her own clumsy way through her angry, helpless tears. She refused to listen to Janaiah who was trying to tell her to come back after four days. Another policeman took her by the arm and dragged her out of the station.

When she returned after a few days, Mumtaz Begum saw that Janaiah was on duty. Her spirits lifted and she approached him hopefully.

'Beta, they will let me see my son today, won't they? When will they set Ahmad free? Did the SI say anything about this?

Janaiah looked troubled. He seemed at a loss for words.

His silence made her grow anxious. 'What is wrong, son? Why don't you say something?'

'When I finished my duty yesterday, Ahmad was still here in the station. But today morning when I came in, I don't see him here. They must have moved him somewhere in the middle of the night ... I don't know where they have taken him ...' Janaiah continued, but Mumtaz Begum was not listening anymore. All these days she was certain, she knew that her son was here, right behind these four walls. Now, they had taken him away somewhere else. She went numb. Her head started spinning and she fell unconscious to the floor with a thud.

The dogs had carried away the little crow.

Translated by **Uma Maheswari Bhrugubanda**

3

Vegetarians Only

We had been walking since morning in this basti. Our legs ached. The soles of our feet burned. We were combing every street and bylane. We had greeted every TO LET board that we had sighted so far. And there were still many more streets left to search. We had covered all the lanes to the right and left of the main road. Of the three houses we had looked at, we liked one very much. It was a small portion of a house. The rent was fifteen hundred rupees a month for one room and a tiny kitchen. In a big city like Hyderabad, it would do for a couple like us. The owner asked us to pay two months' rent as advance. We said we would pay one month's rent now and another after moving in. He agreed. We were hugely relieved, because paying three thousand upfront would have been impossible. We only had fifteen hundred with us right now; so this worked out well. But we were anxious to give him the money immediately. We both had the same thought—we'd be in deep trouble if someone else gave him an advance before we did!

I took out the money and gave it to the owner. He counted it and said, 'All right. When do you want to move in?'

'Right away, sir! We'll bring in some of our things this evening,' I said.

'Okay.' As he turned to go in, the owner paused and asked, 'What is your name?'

My heart sank. I hesitated as we exchanged glances. At that moment I really wished my name was Ramesh or Rajesh or Amit. But there was nothing I could do.

'Yousuf.'

The owner froze as if he had got an electric shock. He blurted out, 'What did you say?'

'I said, *Yousuf*, sir.' I knew then this house, too, was a gone case.

'You are Muslim!' he said in disbelief.

'Yes, we are. But there won't be any trouble, sir. I leave for work early every morning, and she is doing an M. Phil in Telugu.' I was frantically searching for other things to say since what I had said was not going to satisfy the landlord. But I felt there was really nothing more I could say that would please him.

'I thought you were one of *our* people going by the Telugu you spoke. I am sorry but we can't rent out to Muslims,' he said matter-of-factly and tried to return the money he had taken.

Shaheen pleaded, 'Sir, we really like your house. We are very tired with all the searching. We won't trouble you in the least. We are both educated, sir. And we will keep the house neat and clean.'

'I am sorry. My family will not agree.'

I said, 'Sir, why don't you please consult them just once? Please tell them about us. Please ask them to speak to my wife.'

The owner gave me a strange look.

'Please, sir!' I pleaded.

'Okay. Let me see.' He went inside.

I sighed. I was hoping they would agree. We couldn't hear the conversation inside. 'No raised voices. Maybe his wife doesn't mind,' I whispered to Shaheen.

The owner stepped out. 'I'm sorry. They're not willing,' he said, handing back the advance. And he retreated inside without once looking back.

A thorn pierced our hearts once again.

Resigned, I slipped the money back into my pocket and we began our search all over again. We wandered through all the streets in the vicinity, but didn't find a single house that we liked. After a while, we started thinking maybe only Muslims will rent out houses to Muslims. So we set off in the direction of a Muslim locality. I recalled what my friend Shankar had said about Chintalbasti.

'You will find people of all castes and religions there.' Moreover, they were all just ordinary people, what you could call the 'masses'. Not just Muslims but Christians and Jains. People who migrated to Hyderabad from all over the country seemed to be living there, including a large number of Nepalis, he said. Chintalbasti also had a large vegetable market and the weekly general market was on Sundays. So everything was easily available and the bazaar would be bustling with people, mostly from the working class, walking around to buy their daily food and other necessities. All this made Chintalbasti a convenient and attractive proposition.

Immersed in these thoughts, we reached the Muslim neighbourhood in no time. The houses were narrow and small. Poverty announced itself from every corner. Most of the front doors were closed. A few purdahs appeared here and there. A newly built house carried a TO LET board. Our spirits rose. We rang the doorbell. A sweet voice called out in Deccani, 'Kaun hai?'

'We saw the To Let board.'

'Please wait for two minutes.'

'Okay, thanks.'

After a few minutes, the owner emerged, adjusting his lungi. He threw a surprised glance at us. He looked at me and asked, 'Kya karte?'

'I am a journalist and she is studying in the university. It's just the two of us.'

'Are you from Andhra?'

'No,' I replied. 'Why do you ask?'

He gave Shaheen a look of disdain and said, 'You don't wear the purdah?'

'No,' she said in a neutral tone.

'Why?' he asked.

Shaheen was nonchalant. 'Just like that.'

He leaned back against the wall, looked her up and down and said, 'We won't rent our house to people like you.'

I was tempted to retort in that same scathing tone of insult, but controlled myself. Shaheen was bursting with rage and was about to respond when I squeezed her hand to restrain her. The owner continued to stare at us insolently. How we wished we could wipe out that expression from his face! Suppressing our anger and anguish, we stepped out on to the road again.

'No. It is no use. Muslims will not rent us a house. We have to search in the non-Muslim areas. You seem really tired. Why don't you go back to the room? I will search some more,' I said to Shaheen.

After she left, I set out in another direction. I was reminded of a similar incident. Ibrahim was my batchmate at school and also a distant relative. He visited us once when we were living in the Saidabad area. As we were talking over dinner that night, he mentioned that a portion of his mother-in-law's house in Pisalbanda was available for rent. I asked him to inquire whether we could rent the place. And we were shocked by his immediate response: 'My in-laws will not allow people who don't wear the burqa or practice purdah.' I was even more pained when I recalled this incident.

I came to the second main street and entered the first lane. On one side were houses with two and three floors and on the other side were houses with just the ground floor. Those were clearly not houses meant for renting out. So I began to search on the side of the multi-storied buildings. I was excited when I saw a TO LET board hanging from the second floor of the fourth house in that row. I paused near the front gate and looked around. I opened the gate, went inside and rang the bell near the staircase. I walked out again and waited, looking up at the second floor. A woman came out on the first floor balcony and asked me, 'What do you want, babu?'

'It's about the portion to rent, madam,' I said, pointing to the signboard.

'Are you vegetarian or non-vegetarian?' she asked.

I was taken aback. I had never been confronted by such a straightforward question before, and for a few moments, I didn't know how to respond. But of course I couldn't lie. Such truthful beings we are! 'Non-vegetarian, madam.'

'Sorry,' came the instant reply, and she vanished inside.

I felt ashamed of myself ... Or did I feel ashamed of the world? I looked around. Thankfully, there was no one around. I moved on. What exactly did she mean? That they won't rent out to Muslims? No, that was not it. They won't rent out to anyone who was non-vegetarian. So who are those who are purely vegetarian? They would be very few, isn't it? Are these people among those few? And who are non-vegetarians? Think about it—Muslims? Completely non-vegetarian. Christians? Yes. Dalits and the backward castes? Yes, all of them are non-vegetarian. So who does that leave out? The brahmins and the vaishyas! That means the owners must be either brahmin or vaishya, and they will rent their house only to people from their own caste. How remarkable! You can learn so much from just one simple question.

I saw another TO LET sign nearby. I walked towards it hopefully. There was something written beneath the words TO LET. I moved closer wondering what it was. 'Vegetarians Only,' it said. Oh god. This was direct speech. No need for any further information. The board simply said: Get Out!

This lane was of no use. I moved on to the next lane. After another futile search, I left the lane to move into a cluster of houses. There were many houses but none carried any boards. I spotted an old woman sitting on the verandah of a house, chewing betel nut. I approached her and asked, 'Avva, are there any houses around here for rent?'

'That house there, son! That has a portion to rent,' she said pointing to a house. Her words were like music to my ears.

I went to the house and knocked on the door. There was a small gate on the side and I could see part of the house. I waited for some time and knocked again. There was a hand-pump in a corner of the house. A girl stood pumping water into a plastic pot. She was staring at me. I adjusted my hair and looked a little impatiently at the door. I was about to knock once again when the door flew open as if by magic. A stout, light-skinned woman stood in the doorway and threw me a questioning glance.

'Madam, I heard there were rooms for rent.'

'Yes, there are. Are you a bachelor?' she asked.

'No, I'm married. It's just the two of us.'

'You work somewhere? Come in through the side gate,' she said and closed the door on my face.

Thank goodness! She seemed to have some faith in me. I hope the rooms are good. As soon as I opened the gate and went inside, she led me up some stairs. I followed her.

'Where are you living currently?'

'Erramanzil, Balapur, madam,' I replied.

She unlocked the door and stepped aside. 'Take a look,' she said. It was just a single room. There was no washbasin or sink. I asked her about that. She pointed to a small drain hole in one corner of the room. There was a pipe that ran downstairs. She said we should wash there. There was a bathroom and a latrine adjoining the room. That seemed all right, I thought. But I had a doubt, so I asked, 'Are these just for us?'

'No. There are two families living on the other side. These are for common use.'

So those people would come near our door every time they needed to use the bathroom or latrine. This wasn't going to be easy. But what to do! It was already the end of the month and we had to vacate the following day.

'All right. How much is the rent?'

'Fifteen hundred.'

I waited for her to say more. But she didn't ask for a two-month advance. What luck! I was really pleased. I thought to myself that even if it wasn't all that convenient, we ought to adjust and manage in this house somehow.

'Can we move in tomorrow?'

Suddenly, she asked, 'What caste are you?'

My heart sank. What does this mean? How does it matter what caste we were! I wanted to scream that we were just human beings. But she wasn't going to understand. And anyway, no brahmins or reddys were going to come to her house. There would be no hesitation in declaring that one was a reddy. But why was it *so* difficult to say that you were a Muslim? Perhaps it is just as difficult to say that you were mala, madiga or a chakali.

'We are Muslims. My wife did her M.A. in Telugu. We won't be any trouble at all ...' I was going to say more when she dropped another bombshell.

'Do you eat beef?'

How was I to answer this! If I said yes, there was no way she would rent the house to us. What to do? The last time I was asked this question, I shook my head and said 'No', because we desperately needed the place and had nowhere else to go. A month later, the landlord caught me buying beef at a meat shop. Well, what to do? That's the cheapest meat. They abused us really badly that day and asked us to vacate the house instantly. We were shamed in front of the entire neighbourhood. The owners were golla, a cattle-rearing community. One of them almost beat us up. We left immediately and took up another house even though it meant paying extra rent. And now, here was the same question again! I sighed. It was so difficult to live in this world. What did it matter what we ate! But what was I to do now?

'Madam, we do eat beef once in a while. But we won't if you don't want us to. We really do need the house. We've been searching since morning,' I pleaded.

'We won't rent the room to those who eat beef,' she said as she locked up the room.

I stood there not knowing what to say. I had already said we would not eat beef if they didn't like it. What more could I do! I felt like screaming into her ears: The Whole World Eats Cow Meat! But she never even glanced in my direction. She just walked downstairs wordlessly and I was forced to follow her. This entire neighbourhood was going to be useless to me. The girl I had seen earlier was now working the hand-pump vigorously. I felt as if it was aimed at me.

I was back on the road again. I saw the lane leading to the other side of the road. As soon as I walked in, I spotted a two-storied building with a TO LET sign. I rushed to the gate and went inside. There was a staircase on one side and a woman was coming down just then. She looked at me inquiringly. 'There's a sign outside for renting a house,' I said. 'Go inside and speak to the owner. He's in there,' she replied as she left the building.

I went up and saw a big-built man who seemed educated.

'Sir, it's about the house for rent ...'

'How many of you?'

'We are a couple. Just the two of us.'

'The rent is two thousand and two hundred rupees and it includes the electricity and water bill,' he said as he unlocked the house for me. It was a large room and a kitchen. The place had an attached bathroom and was really nice. But the rent was too high.

'Sir, could you reduce the rent, please? My wife is still a student.'

'Well, you are not going to find a house like this in this area for less than twenty five hundred. And I am not even asking you for an advance. Most people would want a two-month advance.'

'You are right, sir. But it's hard to manage with my salary alone. Could you please make it eighteen? We will increase the rent after some time.'

'That's not possible,' he said pausing to think a little. 'Very well. Give me two thousand. You say your wife is still a student. Let's settle it at that. You won't find anything cheaper.'

I started thinking, The house is good and the owner seemed like a nice person. What should I do? Two thousand rupees was a lot of money. Would we be able to manage? It was going to be tough. But we had no choice really. And we were running out of time.

'Very well, sir. I only have fifteen at the moment. Please take this. I will give you five hundred in a couple of days.'

'All right. When do you move in?' he asked as he took the money and counted it.

I was overjoyed to hear this question. 'Tomorrow, sir!'

He said, 'I like educated people. Moreover, you say that it's just the two of you. Keep the house clean. That's all I want.' He didn't ask me anything else. He seemed like the Prophet who had descended upon earth just for me. He hadn't asked which caste I belonged to. Which religion. What I ate. Such a wonderful person! Are there really such people still left in this world? But ... I should tell him that we are Muslims. What if he says 'No' once I tell him this? I had no energy left to begin the search all over again. But it wasn't proper not to tell him.

'Sir, my wife speaks mostly in Telugu. She did her M.A. in Telugu. I work as a journalist in a Telugu newspaper. We are ... Muslims, sir. I hope that is all right,' I said hesitatingly.

'You are Muslim? You don't look like one. You speak such good Telugu!' he said, surprised.

I stood with a forced smile on my face. What was so surprising about speaking good Telugu when we lived in a Telugu state! And is the Telugu language the sole property of Hindus? Or does Urdu belong only to Muslims?

The old man patted my shoulder and left.

Even after a whole week, the mystery of the three questions that the owner did not ask continued to haunt me.

The maid who worked in the neighbouring portion said she would work for us too. After listening to her story, Shaheen agreed to employ her. It was the first time we had a maid in the house. Washing the vessels and clothes and sweeping and mopping the floor, these were her tasks. Two hundred rupees for all this. It was a meagre wage, but it was still a burden for us.

One day while chatting with Shaheen, the maid mentioned the landlord.

'Narsamma, what people are they?' I asked her.

'Arijans,' she said.

So the mystery was finally clearing up. I sank into a chair.

For the brahmins, all non-vegetarians were untouchable. For the shudras, those who ate beef were untouchable. For Muslims, all those who didn't eat halal meat or wear the purdah were untouchable. Who remained outside these equations? In Narsamma's words, only the 'Arijans'—that is, the dalits. And who was untouchable for the dalits? No one!

I closed my eyes. I could see the madigas in my village beating the drums and singing.

Flinch not at the whiplash
Miss not a beat in the tiger dance

Then it dawned on me. With the exception of the dalits, and the madigas in particular, all other castes were in fact untouchable.

Translated by **Uma Maheswari Bhrugubanda**

4

Romance 1424 Hijri

After a round of happy and random browsing at the cyber café, I opened my chat window. I wanted to say hello to Vasu, with whom I had chatted a few times before. I ran through the usual list of names on the chat window. Suddenly, I stopped and scrolled back. There it was, a new name—Sultana! I was surprised. A Muslim woman's name in the chat window?! Wah! It was like spotting a dark cloud on a hot summer day.

I clicked on the name and typed: Salam alaikum! My name is Shafi. Will you accept me as your friend?

No response. What now? My face fell. I spent the next few minutes clicking on some other names. I had always wanted to chat with girls on the chat window, but they stopped responding as soon as I revealed my name. Then I realised that most such feminine names were actually being used by men, and the whole exercise seemed futile. Now here was a real chance. I kept checking on Sultana. A message appeared, saying 'Sultana left the room'. Perhaps Sultana was in the mood to leave when I tried to befriend her, I thought. Bad luck. Since I had already paid my hourly fee, I continued my browsing for the remainder of the hour.

The next day, I went to the café slightly ahead of my usual time. I opened the chat window, entered the chat room and searched for Sultana on the S list. Yahoo! Sultana was there. I clicked on her name, typed out the same request and anxiously waited for her response. It felt great to see Sultana typing out a response, saying: 'As-salam-alaikum. My name is Sultana Anjum. I don't mind being your friend. Please tell me something about yourself.' Ooh! I was so thrilled I didn't feel hungry for the rest of the day!

From that day on, I would reach the cyber café between four and five every evening, no matter what. All my time was spent chatting with Sultana. If I failed to appear on any day, she would ask me why the next day. I was unwilling to tell her that I didn't always have the money, so I would lie and say that I had some work to finish. In the end, I negotiated with the cyber café owner for monthly payment so that I wouldn't miss a single day.

Gradually our conversations grew more intimate, and we would hate to miss out on our chat even for a day. We confessed as much to each other. If one of us didn't make it, the other would sulk. Apologies and much cajoling would follow.

One day I could not help asking her, 'I want to see you. Can we meet somewhere?' She said it was not possible, but she wouldn't give any reasons. She wouldn't even tell me where she was from or what her father's name was. I hoped to find her somehow once I got those details from her. But she stubbornly stuck to her 'No'.

Sultana was a smart girl. She would tease me quite a lot, and get to know so much about me without asking. She could also reveal things about herself, if she wanted to. She could be such a pest sometimes. In one conversation, much to my annoyance, she made me blurt out the name of my village without asking me a single direct question. I had wanted to withhold that information until she had told me where she lived.

'Do you send your sisters to college?' she once asked me. I told her one sister had stopped going, but the other one was studying. 'You have two sisters. Then why aren't you sending the other one to college?' she probed.

On another occasion I asked her, 'Aren't you allowed to talk much at home?'

'I am the talkative one at home. My sister is the quiet type,' pat came the reply.

'Aha. So I have a sister-in-law too,' I quipped.

'Hey, you're crossing your limits,' she warned.

'Forgive me. Please convey my regards to your sister. And if she is a child, please give my kisses to her.' A quarrel promptly ensued. Annoyed with my response, Sultana even refused to tell me her sister's name!

When my dadi died, I could not go to the café for three days. On the fourth day, there was a single question on the computer screen: 'Where were you?' She sulked and refused to accept my explanation. 'Why couldn't you visit the café just once and give me this information? You knew I would wait for you! Do you know how anxious I was? I couldn't sleep at night. Ammi got really worried. Abbu even asked me to stop going to college. But then I wouldn't be able to chat with you, would I?'

'Oh, so you do go to college?' I intervened to distract her.

'Don't tell me you didn't know that until now. How would I come to the café if I were not going to college? You are such a stupid fellow!' She continued to scold me. And I tried in vain to divert her.

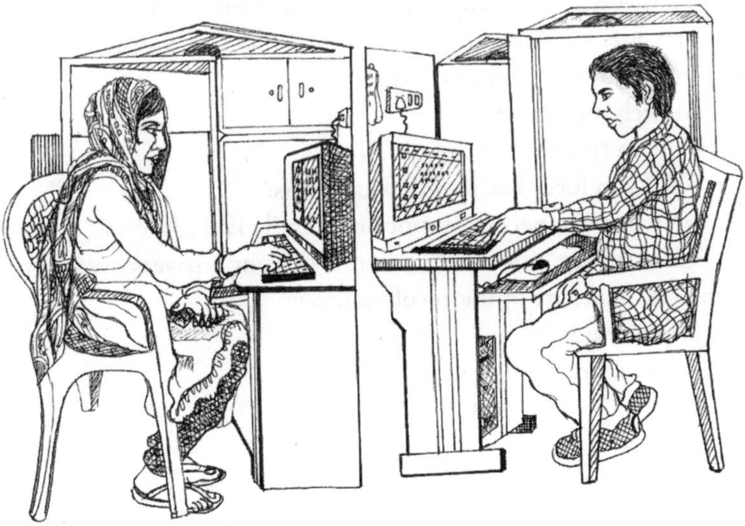

'You can't make me forget my anger by starting a normal conversation. I am not going to speak to you today. You have to do all the talking.' And she fell silent. I had to chat for a whole forty five minutes. She didn't say a word. Before she left, she just typed, 'Khuda hafiz.' I got really mad. The next day, I typed 'As-salam-alaikum' and then sat there for fifteen minutes without saying another word just to annoy her.

Three months passed. I revealed a lot about myself, but could not extract much information about her. She told me that her friend Bhavani, on whose insistence she had come to the cyber café for the first time, was now surprised by Sultana's regular visits. She would talk a lot about things like that.

One day, she wanted me to answer some of her questions. I said I would be happy to.

'Will you seek lein-dein?'

'If your father is in a position to give it, why not!'

'Hey, you are crossing your limits! Remember, I didn't ask you to marry me. Will you allow your wife to take up a job?'

'How can I answer that now?'

'Which means ...?'

'It is up to her.'

'Will you force her to follow customs?'

'That may be necessary since my family is traditional.'

'Chal! What a sly thief you are! All your answers are escapist. Don't you have any opinions of your own?'

'Of course I do!'

'Then tell me.'

'Huh ...?'

'Look at you, trying to think of a response! You don't have any opinions of your own. Because you are a man. You want to enjoy all the privileges that come to men by birth. I can't stand people like you! Bye. See you tomorrow.'

After a few days I asked her again, 'Sultana, I want to see you. Where do you live? I will come and meet you, at any cost.'

'No.'

'Why?'

'I can't tell you. Not now.'

'Are you scared?'

'Shafi, please talk about something else. Our one hour will be up soon.'

'I am desperate to see you, Sultana. I want to discuss this matter right now. That's all.'

'I told you it is not possible now. If you insist, I will leave right now.'

'Acchha, acchha. Why don't you post your photo at least?'

'Oh I see! You want to take the easy way out.'

'Please, Sultana, please!'

'Why don't *you* post your photo?'

'I don't have one ready. If you do it first, I will follow you.'

'No, you do it first. I will do it later.'

'I have to take a photo. I don't have any good photos. It will take time.'

'I have to get a new photo made as well.'

'Please, Sultana.'

'It is fine, Shafi. I will wait till you post your photo. Then I will also post mine.'

'Huth! You are hopeless and stubborn. Wait till we meet.'

After I put up my photo, she teased me for another week. A great deal of persuasion later she promised to put up hers on the day of Jumma. That was three days away. Those must have been the longest three days of my life. The night before Jumma, I found it impossible to sleep. My imagination kept conjuring up Sultana's face in a myriad forms. Even my dreams were full of her.

From the moment I woke up the next morning till it was time to reach the café, the clock seemed to run infinitely slowly. Reaching the café half an hour ahead of my scheduled hour I waited for my turn and felt a sense of calm only after I opened the internet window. But my heart was still racing. Sultana should be beautiful. She should have wonderful eyes, nose and figure etc. etc., I thought to myself. But she hadn't put up her photo yet. She hadn't even come into the chat room. Fifteen minutes passed. I thought that she might not come that day.

Then I saw her 'As-salam-alaikum, Shafi,' and heaved a sigh of relief.

'Why are you so late?'

'A prospective groom's family came to see me today. Relatives visiting my neighbours decided to check me out on the spur of the moment. I wasn't allowed to step out of the house. I had to lie to get out because I knew you would be waiting for me.'

'What happened in the marriage discussions?'

'I don't know. I can't decide.'

'What did you tell them?'

'I didn't say anything. I wanted to wait till I had talked to you.'

'What did you want to ask me?'

'Can we get married?'

'How can I just answer that question? It is so sudden!'

'Do you need time?'

'How much time do you have?'

'Two days. They will come back the day after tomorrow.'

'I will tell you tomorrow.'

'All right. I will wait. But can you decide without seeing me? I have seen you. Even if I hadn't, I would have still liked you. But can you do that?'

'That is what I am trying to do, Sultana.'

'Tell me more.'

'Have you brought your photo? You promised to put it up today.'

'Yes. I took it especially for you. The instructor at this cyber café is a nice girl. I will give it to her to put it up. I have to leave now.'

'Acchha. You give it to her.'

'Khuda hafiz.'

My anxiety increased. I was really tense. After so many months of conjuring up Sultana's face, so many sleepless nights, the moment I had waited for so long had finally arrived. I broke into a sweat, my heart was racing. Please, Allah! She should be a beauty I would instantly fall for. She should have a well-proportioned body. And ... What if she was not good looking?

The photograph slowly started appearing on the screen.

My eyes forgot to blink. I just stared open-mouthed at the computer screen. The photo went chak chak chak, expanding upwards and downwards. First, black hair and a fair forehead. Wah! My heart raced with delight as I realised she was light-skinned.

The forehead expanded. Then I saw the eyebrows ... they were lovely ... then came the eyes ...

What a beauty! Sultana has such beautiful eyes! I wanted to jump for joy. I could feel my face and my heart flooding with happiness. If I were not in a cyber café, I would have surely shouted and sung out loud.

Meanwhile ... Arre! What happened to the photograph? It wasn't progressing any further. The screen seemed to have hung. Damn! Was the computer faulty or was the internet down? Why was the photo turning black from the nose downwards? Then with a shock I realised what it was. I waited until the entire photo had downloaded. Except for her eyes and forehead, the rest of her face was invisible. Sultana had got her photograph taken wearing her burqa and naqab.

It was such a letdown. I felt really cheated!

Translated by **A. Suneetha**

5

The Dying Flame

The fan noisily halted to a stop. The power had gone off again. It must be past midnight. Zareena was staring at the roof sleeplessly, unable to get a grip over her thoughts. Her gaze was steady in the dark. She had gotten used to this kind of darkness for a year and a half now since it first descended on her life.

As it began to get stuffy, her little child stirred restlessly in her bed. Zareena turned on her side to pat her gently back to sleep.

It was two months after this one's birth that Ghouse had got his visa for Saudi. Her body was still stiff from the exhaustion of childbirth and she had been wearing a headscarf. That day, she was feeding the baby when Ghouse had washed his feet and come in. He had sat down next to her, caressed and gently kissed the soft cheeks of the baby. Zareena had smiled at his gesture.

'The date is fixed, Zareen. I leave for Saudi on the tenth.' Her smile vanished. 'So soon? How will I manage with the three children? Fetching water, all the chores outside the house ... How will I cope?' But she did not ask him to stay. She knew of all the travails that Ghouse had suffered to secure a passport and visa.

His mother Bijanbi Phuppamma had put her foot down when Ghouse wanted to make the journey before getting married. 'We will face so many difficulties here!' she had cried. 'Why do you need to go so far across all the seas?' She just would not hear of it. After marriage, he had made a few attempts; but then it was Zareena's turn to oppose, and she had succeeded in stopping him. However, after getting his sisters married, when his newly-married brother separated from the family, Ghouse was left with quite a few debts to clear. With his children, these debts, too, began to grow. He became so anxious that he could no longer eat or sleep properly. It was then that he took the decision to leave everything—his homeland, his children who were very attached to him, his wife who couldn't bear to part with him, his mother, and his friends. How agonising it had been for him to come to that decision!

But it was inevitable. How long could he keep the loan sharks away? How long could he lie to them? His brother bailed himself out by taking a few sensible moneylenders to his side. He was faring all right as a taxi driver. Ghouse took the onus of clearing additional debts in return for the rights over their old house, and this landed him in greater difficulties. The measly salary he earned as a radio mechanic at an electronic shop did not help ease his worries and his troubles only mounted with time.

On some days there was no rice even to cook meals with. To add insult to injury, the moneylenders would often come and scream their guts out in front of his house, demanding their dues in full view of the neighbourhood, leaving Ghouse and his family mortified. On one such occasion, it had caused quite a scene. When one of the moneylenders began to shout at the top of his voice, Ghouse could no longer hold back. 'I don't have any money! What do you want me to do?' That was it! The man caught Ghouse by the scruff of his collar. A fist fight ensued and the neighbours had to intervene to separate the two. 'I am not going to pay you!' Ghouse declared defiantly. 'I will make sure you cough up my money,' retorted the moneylender. The next day, the moneylender organised a panchayati meeting with the community elders. Ghouse was forced to explain his financial condition to them and requested for some more time to repay the loan. The panchayati decided that the money ought to be repaid in a year's time, failing which the house would be auctioned. This stoked the family's fears even more. They shuddered even to think of what would happen if the remaining moneylenders also decided to make a fuss. The only way out for Ghouse was a journey to Saudi to earn money.

Her son's cry for water brought Zareena back to the present. She got up to look for a matchbox to light the lamp, couldn't find it, but managed to fill a tumbler with water in the dark and gave it to the boy. He drank thirstily and mumbled, 'I will sleep now, Ammi.' She laid him down on the bed and caressed his head as he swiftly slid back into sleep.

How Ghouse had loved the boy! How torn he had been to leave him behind! The boy had run a high temperature immediately after his father left for Saudi, and it wouldn't come down. Zareena had been terrified. He would call out for his father in his sleep. It took him quite some time to get used to his father's absence. Before leaving, Ghouse had brought his mother to stay with them, and fortunately, the three children soon grew attached to their grandmother.

The first time he went to Saudi Arabia, Ghouse returned after a year. Allah knows what difficulties he had to face there, but not much money came home that year. What he sent barely sufficed for the household. A measly amount here, a scrap of interest there, and wherever possible they managed to clear a loan with great difficulty.

Bijanbi and Zareena supported and took care of each other throughout the year. As the date of his arrival neared, Zareena longed for the days to pass quickly. They would speak of nothing else but Ghouse. The morning he was to arrive, Zareena swept and cleaned and tidied the house, working round the clock. Every minute seemed like a lifetime.

When he arrived, something about him was different. His words and actions, his face bore a distinct mark of distance. He seemed to have earned well, although he did not say anything to that effect. He cleared off several debts in two days. He partied with friends, but he barely spoke to relatives who came over to exchange pleasantries. He spent most of his time at his Saudi-returned friend, Qasim's house. Zareena noticed all this. Something in his behaviour worried her. 'What is the matter with you, son? You are hardly at home, always out somewhere ...' Bijanbi objected.

One day he came home drunk. He was unhappy and impatient in bed. Zareena had noticed it for too long to keep quiet. 'You have changed,' she said quietly. That led to a fight. 'You have the gall to talk back at me with that ugly face of yours! Whatever I am, put up with it!' he yelled. He said he would kill her if she talked back. She was stunned. She couldn't take it. 'Before you left for Saudi, my face brought you good luck. Now when you have a little money in hand, it has turned ugly?' Their screaming woke up the children, and their startled cries pacified Ghouse somewhat, forcing him to go to sleep. But Zareena couldn't.

After a week, there was another incident. Ghouse's nephew who was a college student had come home that afternoon. Bijanbi was tending to something. The nephew wanted to play with their daughter. So Zareena handed him the girl who was in her arms, responding to something he said with a smile. To Ghouse, who had just entered the house, it seemed as if the young man had briefly embraced Zareena while taking the child from her.

And that was it. The house turned into a battle ground. She was beaten to pulp. Neither Bijanbi nor the children understood what was happening before their eyes. Bijanbi's repeated pleas and attempts to stop Ghouse were of no use. He thrashed Zareena indiscriminately, abusing her all the while. Initially, she couldn't fathom why her husband was beating her. But when his foul language began to make sense, she was stunned. She refused to resist and received his blows passively, until she lost consciousness.

From that day onwards Ghouse stopped coming home. Bijanbi went searching for him to Qasim's house. She begged him, 'Zareena is not what you take her to be, Ghouse. Why do you accuse her of such a grave crime? Haven't you kept me here to watch over the family? I have been watching her, haven't I? It is true that the boy came home a couple of times, and I was the one who invited him. We were just two women and could not manage all the errands we needed to run. He could not refuse. He is a good boy, not the kind you think he is. Why are you behaving this way? Be reasonable. Listen to me, son, I am your mother, Ghouse! *Listen* to me!' But all her entreaties fell on deaf ears. Finally, in desperation, she cursed him thoroughly and returned home in utter distress.

Zareena was inconsolable. 'It is fine if he beats me. But how could he accuse me of infidelity! What wrong have I done, Phuppamma?' She sobbed endlessly in Bijanbi's lap that day.

There was no one to question or reason with Ghouse. Much to her dismay, Zareena came to know that some neighbours had apparently said, 'How long can wives wait when husbands leave them for months and years? Won't they look to others!' A week before Ghouse was to return to Saudi, she received the shocking news that he was going to marry a relative of Qasim. She almost collapsed. There were many altercations in the family. Some advised Zareena to lodge a case against him. But she did nothing of the sort. She had never dreamt that Ghouse would do something like this. Her despair grew. She turned into a lifeless wreck. Bijanbi could not digest this news either. She went over to Qasim's house and abused Ghouse to her heart's content.

Those were such miserable gloomy days. Bijanbi was shattered. She would cling to the children and cry. Distraught at the injustice meted out to her daughter-in-law, she took ill and was soon bedridden. Within four months, she died. There was little doubt that it was her grief and worry about Zareena and the children's future that consumed her. During her illness, even when her younger son invited her to come and stay with him, she did not leave Zareena. She told Zareena several times not to inform Ghouse when she died.

That night before her death, Bijanbi refused to swallow even a morsel. In the morning, her cheeks bore the stains of tears and her eyes were lifeless. Zareena would never forget that image for the rest of her life. Her brother-in-law came and took the body to his house. She followed the family, weeping. By the time of zohar namaz, they carried the body to the masjid. Zareena returned home after dark. No one asked her to stay. Everyone was cold and kept their distance.

Without Bijanbi Phuppamma, Zareena became lonelier. The thought of suicide crossed her mind several times. But the sight of her children always stopped her.

Zareena was brought back to the present once more with her daughter's cry. The girl was still asleep, but it was getting stuffy in the small room. Zareena was sweating profusely. It looked like the power would not come back anytime soon. She found her way in the dark and opened the main door. A waft of cool breeze entered bringing some respite, but the mosquitoes would not leave them in peace. The alley was dark and quiet. When the little girl began to wail again, Zareena lifted her up and carrying her against her shoulder, paced in and out of the house.

The older boy called out, 'Ammi ...'

'What is it?'

'Ammi, I am scared.'

'Why? What is there to be scared of? I am here. Go back to sleep. I can't find the matches to light the lamp. Go back to sleep. I am right here.'

On his last visit, Ghouse had wanted to see the older boy. His friend Jameel had come over and taken the boy to his house. Ghouse had chatted with him for a long time. He had asked if his mother was looking after them well. He had given him a thousand rupees and promised to go to the boy's school the next day and pay his fees. Zareena felt disturbed by all this. She did not know whether she wanted to see him or not. She was restless. In a month, Ghouse left. She gathered there were problems in his new marriage. Six months later, she learnt that his new family was after his money and was constantly making demands for more. So he stopped all communication with the new family, too; no calls, no letters.

After a whole year had passed, yesterday, Zareena received a letter from Ghouse. She was overwhelmed by a mix of emotions. Was it surprise, was it joy, hope or dismay, she did not know. Her eyes welled up as she read the two lines: 'Zareen, I have been thinking of you and the children. I am coming on the twenty-fifth.'

When dawn breaks, it would be the day of his arrival. Zareena could not sleep. She did not know what time it was. Her heart was heavy. The little girl cried as soon as she lay her down in bed again. Zareena felt something rustle underneath the pillow. Then she remembered. She had kept it there the previous night. She felt for it in the dark and took out the box of matches from under the pillow. She struck a match and lit the small lamp. There wasn't much oil left in it.

She did not know how long the light would last.

Translated by **Kiranmayi Indraganti**

6

Homeland

Sultan was restless ever since Yadaiah had called to inform him that Suresh was coming back. He found it difficult to sit in his shop. All kinds of thoughts came to him, all kinds of faces flitted past his mind and memories came flooding back. Restless, he got up and came out of his shop. He looked up and down the lane that was studded with rows of shops. All of them were teeming with customers, all except for his shop which wore a deserted look.

He looked at his shop. There were cobwebs in every corner. Old and unsold television and radio sets, tape-recorders and various other articles were covered with dust. A strange smell emanated from his shop, a smell that came from old equipment that hadn't been cleaned for years, a smell of old and unused electronic goods. Sigh! He couldn't take it anymore. Sultan was overwhelmed by a peculiar fear, a fear that seemed to have no reason or basis. He felt a burning sensation in his stomach. Could it be hunger? He wasn't sure. What should he do now? He went inside, took the keys and came out. He pulled down the shutter, locked it and climbed down the steps in front of his shop. But his legs seemed impossibly heavy. They seemed weighed down by his thoughts and the many different scenes that were playing out in front of his eyes.

Ten years ... In just ten years, how had his life changed so drastically? Ten years ago, he was on a high—he had a house, he had a shop that did good business. How did things come to such a pass in just ten years? Misfortune seemed to have caught him in a relentless, ever-tightening grip. Was it just his misfortune, or did he not do the right things at the right time? Was it because of the circumstances in which his community found itself, or was it something in his culture?

After he returned from Dubai, Sultan bought a motorbike and various other expensive things for his house. He set up this shop of electronic goods and stocked cassette players, TV and radio sets. Business took off to a flying start. He was much feted and admired by everyone. There was no end to visits from relatives and to demands made on him by siblings. And then in just two or three years, all that he had earned and saved had evaporated. He was left with just his shop and his wife Shaheen's jewellery to fall back on. With the arrival of computers, VCDs and DVDs, soon there were few takers for radios and cassette players. Nobody even brought them for repair anymore. People stopped asking for assembled TV sets. The question of stocking branded goods did not arise as he wasn't making enough even to feed his own family. Slowly, ever so slowly, his business began to slide. He could no longer afford to employ helpers in the shop. The expensive goods that he had bought for his house, as well as Shaheen's jewellery, all went one by one. He couldn't save his precious motorbike either. Just the other day, he was forced to sell it to pay the rent for his shop.

Sultan suddenly saw a motorbike coming straight at him and panicked. He moved aside just in time to avoid the speeding bike. The shiny Hero Honda whizzed past him. He kept staring at it. No, actually it was Sultan himself who was speeding away on the bike. He zoomed towards his house and brought the bike to a screeching halt at his doorstep. He honked as he got off the bike and put it on its stand. He could hear the tinkling of his little daughter's anklets from inside as tiny feet came pattering to the door. 'Munni, be careful or you will fall!' he called out. He could hear his wife running and picking up Munni before she opened the door for him. As she held the curtain aside to let him in, he could see two faces radiant as the moon, and behind them, his moonlit world.

Where has all that gone? He stood in front of the closed door and rattled the latch. There were no sounds from within the house. He waited and soon he heard soft footfalls. Shaheen opened the door. His moon seemed to have lost its glow. Her neck was bare, no necklace of moonstone adorned it. His moonlit world, too, was lost. Everything seemed empty and lacklustre. Everything he once possessed was lost.

'What happened? Why are you late today?' Shaheen asked. 'Nothing,' he replied. He washed his hands and feet and relaxed on the couch. His daughter Munni and son Chand had gone to school. Shaheen spread the straw mat on the floor and placed the dastarkhan on it. She served him his food. 'What happened? Are you not feeling well?' she asked. She touched his forehead to see if he was running a fever. Sultan could feel his eyes welling up. How difficult it was to keep anything from his wife!

After his meal, Sultan went back to the shop. After an hour or so, the phone rang. It was Yadaiah. 'Sultan, you are coming, right?' he asked.

'I cannot come, ra ... I have some work,' said Sultan.

'Come on! Suresh will be really upset if you don't! He will wonder what is so important that Sultan can't come to see me? Remember, we gave him such a grand send-off when he was leaving. Now you don't want to see him when he has returned after so many years!' admonished Yadaiah.

'I don't know why I don't feel like coming, ra. Please don't force me. You all go.'

'Come on, Sultan! Have you forgotten the grand welcome Suresh organised for you when you returned from Dubai?'

'Please bhai, leave me alone,' Sultan said and hung up the phone.

He felt extremely restless. He did want to meet Suresh. But at the same time, he didn't. He could not put his finger on the reason. What was it? Was it his present circumstances? Or was it something else that bothered him? The memories of his return from Dubai hadn't faded. Suresh had indeed been at the heart of the celebrations. He and other friends had brought Shaheen, Chand and Sultan's mother to the airport. His father, his younger sisters Waheeda and Shahida, his brothers-in-law and younger brothers, everyone was there.

Sultan had so looked forward to seeing his family again that he did not know whom to greet first once he got off the flight. He had broken down on seeing his mother, hugging her tightly through his sobs. Shaheen and his sisters had put their arms around him and wept with joy. Before he left, Sultan had never lived away from his family for even a day. But he had gone to Dubai. And he had returned after five long years. The tears would not stop. Sultan had warmly exchanged alai-balai with his best friends Suresh and Yadaiah, his father and his brothers, embracing each of them in turn. Then they had all set out for home. Everyone had stayed back at his house that night. The celebrations continued. Suresh had insisted on honouring Sultan and Shaheen with huge garlands of flowers, and feeding them sweets. In response to Sultan's protestations, Suresh had said, 'Why, it is my pleasure! Didn't your family give you a grand farewell? I want your return to be celebrated in style, too!' Overcome by emotion, the two friends had embraced each other. The three of them did not sleep a wink that night. Suresh and Yadaiah had filled in Sultan on developments in Nalgonda in the five years of his absence. They told him in turns about each of their friends and acquaintances and how each one was now 'settled' in life.

And then Suresh had casually announced that he too had got his passport done. Sultan was astonished. 'What are you saying, Suresh? When I decided to leave for Dubai, didn't you take me to task? Where is the need to go to a foreign land, you had said. We can make a living right here in our own country. You also told me that you loathed such people and that you would never ever do such a thing in your life. You had made fun of Muslims who made a beeline for Dubai and the Gulf. Are you not doing the same yourself now?' Sultan had angrily responded.

'Actually, it was my father and uncles who insisted,' Suresh said hesitantly.

Sultan had exploded. 'Don't give excuses, bhai! If you are not convinced yourself, how can anyone force you to do such things! So at least now you must accept that it is not wrong to go in search of opportunities in foreign countries, to build a better future for ourselves and our family.'

'No, no. I still believe it is wrong to leave one's motherland. I wonder how people can abandon their native place to go to some far-off land ...' Suresh trailed off.

'It is not a question of right or wrong. Circumstances compel people like us to leave. But you have no such compulsions. And yet your folks want you to go so far away! Can't you see the difference between people like you and us?' retorted Sultan.

'What is the difference?'

'Of course, there is a difference! When I first mooted the idea of going to Dubai, everyone in my family had opposed it. But it was clear that I would not find a job here. And the moneylenders were giving us all sleepless nights. The future seemed utterly bleak. So we had to take this difficult decision. But look at you! You may not be so keen to go, but your parents want you to go. They insist that you go. *That* is the difference.'

'Okay, that is the example of only one person. But isn't it true that many Muslims want to go to Dubai?' asked Suresh.

'Oh God! How to explain that to you now? The entire community is in the same situation as my family. No one chooses to leave, Suresh. There is no joy in leaving behind your loved ones—your wife, your children, your parents and siblings and friends. It is especially hard to leave the land of your birth and cross the seven seas to go to a strange, foreign land. In my community, often the entire household depends on the earnings of just one person. There are sisters to be married off, aged and infirm parents to be taken care of, and younger brothers like me who cannot find any decent employment. There are so many problems a family faces! Can't you understand these things? Do Muslims own agricultural land? Do they have any traditional occupations? Do they have reservations? How long do you want us to stick to petty roadside businesses? We eat when we can earn, or else we go hungry,' Sultan had passionately argued.

Sultan was jolted back to the present when he heard his neighbour pulling down the shutters of his shop. He too switched off the lights, downed the shutter noisily, locked up the shop and began to walk home.

Two days later, Sultan was sitting in his shop as usual, lost in thought, when Suresh walked in. Sultan couldn't believe his eyes.

'What's this, Sultan? You didn't come to see me even though you knew I was back!' Suresh said, almost accusing him. Sultan got up and embraced him warmly. 'How have you been, ra? It's been so long since we met!' As they gazed at each other, holding the other tightly by the shoulders, the two men were overwhelmed by emotion. Neither hid his tears, nor let go of the other for a long time. They inquired after each other's wellbeing at length, still holding hands. Sultan briefly stepped out of the shop and ordered tea for both of them. As they sipped the sweet hot tea, Suresh began to talk of his life in the USA.

Sultan listened to him somewhat absentmindedly for a while. Then he heard Suresh saying, 'I just got my green card ... My wife is pregnant, you know, and we plan to have the baby there so that our child will be an American citizen ...'

Sultan heard no further. He got up and grabbed Suresh by the collar of his shirt and began to shout at the top of his voice, 'What, mister? Do you remember how you made fun of me when I was leaving for Dubai? How you had mocked me? Do you remember how you said it was so easy for Muslims to break away from their land of birth and go to the Gulf and Dubai because they did not consider this land to be their own and because they did not love their country? Do you remember? Here you are, born in this land, and choosing to settle down in the USA. Gloating over your green card, planning with great joy and anticipation the birth of your child in that foreign land so that he can be born an American citizen. Can Muslims ever dream of going to America? No. They go to countries like Dubai and slog like dogs in jobs that no one else wants to do there. They are separated from their families for years together; they are deprived of the comfort of a wife, the love of parents and children. They have no one to care for them in that alien land when they fall sick. And if they die there, their families can't even afford to bring back the body for burial in the land of their birth. We go there in search of a livelihood, but our hard-earned money comes back to this country, doesn't it? Whereas you gain your degrees here, but prefer to settle down in countries like America. We, who have no worthwhile education, work as labourers and bring in valuable foreign exchange for our homeland. And no matter how long we work abroad, we always return ... to our homeland.'

Suresh stood up abruptly. He shook Sultan by the shoulder and asked, 'Sultan, what happened to you? You have suddenly become so silent. Why are you so distracted, ra?' Sultan was forced out of his reverie. He shook his head and smiled a mirthless smile.

Translated by **R. Akhileswari**

7

The Benefactor

How am I going to manage this wedding, Fatima asked herself for perhaps the hundredth time. Walking briskly against the blazing red sun in a black burqa, she was already drenched in sweat. She had been walking for about fifteen minutes now. By the main road, she would have had to change two autos. One autorickshaw on the straight two-kilometre road, followed by another kilometre to the left in a second autorickshaw. It would probably cost her ten rupees in all—five rupees each way. Instead, if she took the narrow dust track, it would only be two kilometres across. It would be a half-an-hour walk at most, Fatima told herself, and set off. She was headed to her brother Zameer's place.

It was an unusually hot day. The heavy fabric of her sari and blouse made things worse. On top of that, the black burqa—her clothes were soggy with sweat. Fatima wondered if Zameer was at home. It was Sunday. He should be home. He *must* be home. She had pinned all her hopes on him. He understood and he empathised. He would help her. If only he agreed to support her, she would find it so much easier to ask the others for help. But *would* he? If only this one task was behind her, she could breathe and relax a little.

It was too good an alliance to let go of. Ameena Khala was aware of Fatima's circumstances; she had somehow convinced the boy's family to accept their proposal. Ameena had said again and again that it would be very difficult to find such a good match for such a small dowry. So Fatima told herself, come what may, she will not lose this opportunity. She hurried on. She had made it past the halfway point. Clouds of dust rose in the wake of every passing vehicle as she walked along the unpaved road.

Gausiya was already twenty. Four years ago, Gausiya's father had begun searching for grooms. But he died suddenly without seeing it through. Goddamn heart attack—it just came out of nowhere! Fatima had pleaded, 'Are you in pain? Let's go to the hospital!' But he wouldn't listen. 'It is just a waste. Nothing will come of it. They will only charge us an arm and a leg for all the new problems they will find.' And he lost his life before he could be taken to the hospital, right in front of their eyes. That is when her troubles began. For the past four years, not one good night's sleep had she got. Nor seen a day without hunger; no peace of mind either. She was at her wit's end trying to run the household and raise three daughters. How was she ever going to get each one of them married? What an insurmountable task it seemed! She had been trying for the last two years to get the eldest one married. She had come to understand that it was near impossible to get a girl married these days. Everyone was asking for lakhs. Even a rickshawallah demanded seventy or eighty thousand. How could she sleep? Constant worry about her daughters' marriage made her restless, anxious, even desperate. There were times that she thought of putting an end to everything by poisoning her daughters and herself.

Seeing that the road was empty, Fatima paused briefly to untie the naqab and wipe the sweat off her face. She tied it again and continued on her way. She finally got off the dust track and onto the paved road. She should reach soon.

If her daughters had done well in their studies, someone or the other would have offered to marry them. But they did not. The eldest was the worst. Their father died when the second one was in eighth grade and the youngest in sixth. Fatima had to put an end to their education from then on. Of course, there was no way the girls could go out and work. So they stayed at home and did what they could to run the household. The eldest was good with the sewing machine and the younger ones, with hand stitch. But what they earned was hardly enough to buy clothes and medicines. Fatima had never seen or touched a five hundred or a thousand rupee note. How was she going to pay for the weddings?

At last, she stood in front of Zameer's door and rang the doorbell. His wife Rehana opened the door. 'Salam alaikum, Apa! Please come in,' she said.

'Is Zameer home?' asked an anxious and exhausted Fatima as she walked in, removing her naqab.

'He is, Apa. I'll just let him know that you have come. Please have a seat,' Rehana said as she went into the bedroom.

Zameer came out. 'Salam alaikum, Apa.'

'Valaikum salam,' Fatima responded as she sank into a chair. She was relieved to see him.

'How are the children, Apa?' Zameer asked.

'They are fine,' Fatima said, taking the glass of water from Rehana.

'Take off your burqa and wash your hands and feet. Have lunch with us.'

'No, Zameer, I should go. I also need to go to Kaleem's place, and then there are so many other chores.'

'What is the matter, Apa? You look anxious.'

'Ameena Khala has brought a rishta for Gausiya. The boy works in a cell phone shop. A smart boy. The family is poor like ours. They want at least fifty thousand as dowry so that even if they spend twenty on the wedding, he would still be left with thirty thousand to set up a small business. In fact, they initially wanted eighty thousand. But Ameena strongly recommended Gausiya and somehow persuaded them to bring it down to fifty, explaining our family's situation. So you see, our Gausiya could be married off for fifty thousand! If we let this rishta go, we will find it very difficult later. We should get it done, Zameer, come what may. I will go plead with each one of our relatives to help. I will not be able to sleep unless I get her married. I really need you to stand by me. My hopes now rest on you, Zameer. Please don't say no!' Fatima was breathless with anxiety. She looked like she would burst into tears any moment now.

Just then Rehana came in and handed them a hot cup of tea each. Zameer sipped his tea in pensive silence. He knew his sister wouldn't take no for an answer. He thought it over. It was going to be difficult. Nevertheless, he decided to do more than his share.

'Don't worry, Apa. We should make all efforts on our part. Above and beyond that, there is Allah. It is true that I have been in some difficulties of late. Even so, I will not back off when you need me. I will do whatever I can within my capacity. Just tell me what I have to do,' he said determinedly.

Fatima's face relaxed. She put down her tea cup. 'You say you have some problems ... I leave it to you, Zameer. I am sure you will do the right thing.'

'I can arrange for five or six thousand from my side. And if you still need more, I can borrow up to two, three thousand more from someone. This is what I can manage,' he said, slowly working things out in his mind.

Fatima was heartened. 'I am so glad to hear you say this, Zameer. With your assurance and support, I will make this wedding take place even if I have to run around till my slippers wear out. If only Gausiya's father was still around, it wouldn't have been so hard ...' Fatima said, her voice choking.

Zameer got up and walked over to her. 'Nakko ro, Apa ... Hum hain na! Please don't cry. We are there with you. Everything will be fine. Allah is with us. Don't worry.' Rehana also chimed in, 'Nakko ro, Apa!'

Fatima wiped her tears. 'Acchha, I must go now. Ameena Khala said I have two days to decide. I will also speak to Kaleem. I should leave,' Fatima said and got up.

'Apa, just wait a minute,' Zameer said and he went inside. Fatima put on her naqab. Zameer returned with a couple of fifty rupee notes and handed them to her. 'Go back in an autorickshaw. Don't go walking to everyone's house, Apa.'

Fatima looked up at him gratefully and nodded. Zameer and Rehana walked out with her to see her off.

From one end of the town, Fatima reached her other younger brother's house to the north of the town. Her sister-in-law Khatija insisted that Fatima take off her burqa and helped her wash her hands and feet. Just then Kaleem returned home. He washed, changed clothes and sat down. He asked after his sister's wellbeing. Khatija spread the dastarkhan meanwhile and laid out the food. Their three children had gone to their uncle's place, she said.

Fatima sat down next to Kaleem and she told him about the proposal for Gausiya. She wasn't as fervent as she had been with Zameer, but she stressed that Kaleem should try and help as best as he could. That was it. Kaleem must have been under some duress for he nearly shouted back at her, 'From where am I going to get the money, Apa? Just sending these three to school costs a chunk! We have already taken a loan this year. Your husband left behind three daughters. Who is going to arrange for their marriage? It is not within our capacity. You can do whatever you like.'

Khatija intervened sharply, 'That is no way to talk to your elder sister!'

Fatima was overcome with a sudden sadness. Despite Khatija's protests, she grabbed her burqa and quickly left the house.

It was the morning of the fifth day. Fatima was hurrying along in her burqa when she saw Saleem coming towards her on a bicycle. 'Apa! Where are you off to so early?'

'I'm going to Devarakonda, Saleem. Tayaba's son, my cousin brother lives there. I am going to tell them about Gausiya's proposal.'

'Apa, wait! I will drop you off at the bus stand,' Saleem said as he got off the cycle and turned it around.

'That won't be necessary, Saleem, I'm all right,' Fatima said, walking on.

'No, no, Apa. Please sit behind me on the cycle,' he insisted, adjusting his cap. He helped Fatima sit on the carrier and climbed onto his seat from the front. 'How far have your efforts reached, Apa?'

'I need another twenty thousand, Saleem. I don't know how I will make up the rest. That is why I am going to Devarakonda. To ask if my cousin can help.'

Saleem was silent for a while. As they reached the crowded bus stop, he said, 'Safe journey, Apa. Allah will see to it that your work is accomplished.' Fatima got off and he turned to go back.

She asked for directions to the Devarakonda bus bay. Then she walked up to another person and asked him, 'Is this the bus for Devarakonda?' She got in and found a window seat. After a few minutes, the driver took his seat. As the bus began to move, her thoughts, too, moved on.

Saleem was a nice boy. She liked him. Their house was a couple of houses away. She had broached the topic with his mother. But she had said, 'Saleem doesn't want to get married, Fatimabi! He wants to devote his entire life to Islam. What do I do!' It was true. He was forever wandering around the villages, talking to folks about Ijtema. He let his beard grow. He never took his cap off. He was always seen in his white lalchi pajamas. Absolutely devoted to reading his namaz five times a day. In fact, namaz, Allah and Islam were the only things on his mind. No this-worldly topic appealed to Saleem. Well, to each his own, I suppose.

Fatima had also broached the topic with Iqbal's mother, the neighbour across the street. 'We have taken a lot of loans to send our son to study computer science. He is already getting proposals from people who know that he is guaranteed to get a good job. Some are even willing to give him expensive gifts and cash in lakhs. Why would he marry *your* daughter?' Iqbal's mother had dismissively said. It saddened Fatima to recall her words even now.

These past few days, she had been getting around quite a bit. Zameer's assurance and encouragement had cheered her up. But Kaleem's dispiriting response had sunk her hopes. She had gone home crying after leaving Kaleem's place. That night, she went to bed without eating. When the children tried to wake her up, she curled up in bed and said she wasn't feeling well. By the end of the day, however, Kaleem had sent his eldest son to her with five thousand rupees.

Fatima had woken up early the next morning, completed all her chores, and gone to see her two younger sisters. The older one's husband, Khaja Mian, was a good man. He promised three thousand by the time of the wedding, plus two sets of clothes for each of the girls. Her youngest sister's husband, Ghouse Pasha, also pledged two thousand. She approached two other relatives in the same town, and they both pledged a thousand each. Another relative had pleaded, 'I am in no state to help you, please forgive me.' The next day, she approached Gausiya's paternal uncles. They pledged three thousand each. One early morning, she went in search of a Saudi-returnee's house. Word had it that he helped poor girls to get married. He promised her five thousand and asked Fatima to come with a rokkha before the wedding.

Zameer's eight thousand; Kaleem's five thousand; brothers-in-laws' five thousand; six thousand in all from Gausiya's paternal uncles; two thousand from two relatives; the Saudi man's five thousand—all this added up to thirty-one thousand. But she needed twenty more. Who else could she possibly ask? The cousin in Devarakonda was running two lorries for business. She would have to ask him for a substantial amount.

The bus came to a halt. Fatima bought a dozen bananas and went looking for the house. After a few inquiries and some searching, she found it at last. She was dumbstruck. What all had she heard, and what now stood before her—a small dilapidated rented hovel. She couldn't believe her eyes. She knocked on the door. A woman opened the door. Fatima told her she had come all the way from Nalgonda and that Maqsood Bhai was her cousin. She was ushered into the house. Maqsood Bhai was in bed. He appeared to have been bedridden for quite some time. Fatima was surprised and saddened.

'As-salam-alaikum, Bhai! I am Fatima, your uncle's daughter,' she said, raising her voice a little as she came closer. The sunken eyes wearily scanned her face, searching for family resemblance. He was barely able to talk.

The woman gave Fatima some water. 'What happened to him?' Fatima asked.

'Drinking, Apa! He got addicted to it ever since we bought the lorries. We incurred losses from the lorries. After doing so well for ourselves, we ended up like this,' she said, sobbing quietly.

Fatima sat down next to the woman and tried to comfort her as best as she could. She knew nothing would come of it. But what else could she do? She couldn't bear looking at the two of them. She kept some money for the bus journey and put the rest—sixty rupees—into the woman's hands and bade them goodbye.

Later that day, Ameena Khala brought along Masooda, the boy's mother. Fatima ran around fixing up the place. She spread the mat and a clean bed sheet on the floor for them to sit on. She served them tea and asked them to stay for lunch. She told her daughters to cook another cup of rice.

Masooda nudged Ameena Khala, who coughed politely and asked, 'How far have you reached, Fatima? How much have you managed to collect? Will you be able to give fifty? Masooda thinks that once we sort that out, we can discuss the rest.'

Fatima felt a little tightness in her chest. She said, 'Khala, you know my situation quite well. From the time you mentioned this rishta, I have just been running from house to house, rounding up pledges. So far I have thirty thousand. With a little more time, I can make the fifty.'

'It won't do, amma. We cannot wait longer. We waited this additional week purely on Ameena's insistence. But you have only thirty thousand. We have been approached thrice already by another party willing to give fifty and also pay for a good wedding.

Our son is in a hurry. It is not up to us to wait anymore. I am sorry. Do not think ill of us,' Masooda said matter-of-factly and got up to leave.

Fatima felt as if a huge invisible boulder had descended onto her chest and she couldn't breathe. She rose and caught Masooda's hands in her own, pleading, 'Please don't say that, Apa! Your proposal had brought such high hopes. Please don't dampen them. Try and understand my plight. Please give me just one more week and I assure you I will have everything arranged. Or else, take the thirty thousand now and let the wedding go through. Once it is over, you will get all your dues, I promise. Please don't say no, Apa! Show a little generosity. Please be a little more patient for our sake.'

'I am sorry, we cannot wait any longer. Maaf karna!' Masooda said, withdrawing her hands from Fatima's clasp.

Ameena tried to negotiate. 'Oh dear! Who is going to understand poor people's problems if not for poor people? After her husband died, Fatima has had a really hard time managing the house and three young girls. Please, you must be a little more understanding ...'

'I can't believe you too are talking like this, Khala! You know that my boy has been pressing me to finalise this quickly. A man he knows is willing to sell a cell phone repair shop for thirty-five thousand. My son wants that at any cost—he is insistent. I cannot wait any longer. I cannot be bothered,' Masooda said and walked out.

'Masooda ... Masooda! Please listen ...!' Ameena went after her.

'Apa, Apa, rukiye ... Apa!' Fatima pleaded. But Masooda had left.

Stunned, Fatima stood still. The two younger girls came up to her and looked at their mother's face anxiously. Inside, in the kitchen, Gausiya's eyes filled with tears. She stood leaning her head against the wall, scratching it with her nails.

'Let it go, dear. What can we do? It is not in our kismat. It will take place according to Allah's will. He knows. He understands everything. He alone will look after us. Don't worry. I will come again. My daughter-in-law and grandchildren are visiting. I had come this way with Masooda. I will see you again, bidda,' Ameena Khala said, and covering her head with one end of her sari, she left.

An immense sorrow engulfed Fatima. She collapsed on the reed mat and began to weep uncontrollably. Seeing their mother so broken and distraught, the two younger daughters also started sobbing. Gausiya came out of the cooking hovel and fell upon the mat next to her mother. They both held each other tightly and cried out aloud. Their wails carried outside. The puzzled neighbours came out of their houses to see what was happening. Fatima's house was soon full. But they couldn't stop crying. The women tried hard to console and comfort Fatima and her daughters. 'What happened?' the men asked. No one had a clue. Lateef from next door, Jani Mian from across, Qasim from two doors away—everyone enquired. Saleem also joined the crowd. Wiping the tears from her own eyes, old Nani from next door said, 'What happened? These days one can't find niyat anywhere. No one cares for the worries of the poor anymore. Her man died. The woman has piles of hardship. People are asking for dowry in lakhs to marry the eldest daughter. Is this an acceptable custom in our Islam? A recent proposal asked for a minimum of fifty thousand. The poor woman wandered about asking for help till her slippers wore out. She couldn't get it done. Now she cannot bear it anymore after they rejected her. Who is going to look after the poor? Damn this world!'

Everyone was moved by the plight of Fatima and her daughters. Every time someone tried to console them, the women wailed louder. The crowd swelled.

Then, in the midst of it all, moving like a white pigeon, Saleem stepped forward and spoke with a quiet confidence, 'Fatima Apa, I will marry Gausiya. I don't want a single paisa for dowry. I will have the nikah read in the masjid tomorrow. Now wipe your tears, Apa.'

For a while, no one understood what Saleem had said. Once it finally sunk in, the tears flowing down Fatima's cheeks turned into tears of joy. Fatima got up, walked up to Saleem and wordlessly took both his hands and raised them to her eyes as if in worship.

Translated by **Christopher Chekuri**

8

The Wedding Feast

Our friendship was the envy of Keshurajupally village. Everyone was amazed at how close the three of us were. Whatever we did, wherever we went, we were together. If anyone in the village had any business with any one of us, they just needed to ask either of the other two about the third one's whereabouts, and they were sure to get the information. We were inseparable. If we did not meet even for a day, it seemed as if we hadn't met for ages. Whenever we went to get our clothes ironed, chakali Ishwaramma made it a point to ask, 'The three of you are so close. Will you always be like this?' And one of us would invariably respond, 'Why not? We will always be together.' Ishwaramma would not be convinced. 'I am not so sure. Once you get married and have a wife, this relationship will not be the same. Just you wait and watch. I have seen so many like you.' She was not the only sceptic. Many others would voice similar doubts about our dostana. It was no different with our families. Initially, they did not approve of it. 'How can you be friends with those kafirs!' was the question I often faced from my family. Narendar Reddy's family would similarly object, 'What's this friendship of yours with that Turka fellow?'

But I continued to visit my friends' houses without any hindrance or hesitation. I ate with them, slept in their house, and of course, we talked endlessly. My house was small and it was always crowded, with my two sisters, my brother, my mother, father and myself, all living under one roof. Therefore, my friends could not come to my house often. Even if they did, I would immediately leave with them. As for Parashuram, he met us mostly on the road. We would meet up at Lingamma's hotel and then roam about together, perfectly happy in each other's company.

That particular summer, it so happened that marriages were fixed in both Narendar's family and mine. They were due to be celebrated within days of each other. In Narendar's house, it was his younger sister getting married, and in my house, it was my elder brother. Our houses soon became hives of activity. There was so much to be done! And of course, there was our usual roaming around together which we wouldn't want to miss at any cost.

My brother's wedding was the first to take place. We had to put up the wedding pandal in front of my house. The three of us, along with other friends, went to the village pond, cut a few sarkar trees and used their trunks as poles for the pandal. Then we got some sheaves of dried millet grass and branches of the vayil tree for the roofing. Within three days, the pandal was up. Then we put up a similar one in front of Narendar's house. At the end of each day, we were dog-tired and went to the palm groves to relax with glasses of toddy.

The three of us divided up the various tasks that had to be completed for the weddings. Each of us put our heart and soul into all the preparations as if the wedding was in our own family. Take my brother's wedding, for instance. All of us went together to attend the nikah ceremony in Suryapet. We thoroughly enjoyed the dinner that followed. Since we belonged to the groom's side, we also threw our weight around. During the jalwa ceremony when the bride's face is shown to all the guests by turns, oh how we ragged the bride's family! We cracked jokes by the dozen. Parashuram supplied us with a steady flow of wisecracks which we bandied as our own before the guests and the bride's family. At the end of it all, we left for our village, taking the bride with us.

The next day, we had to organise the walima dinner. By evening we had put up an additional tent in front of our house and arranged chairs for the guests. Preparations for the dinner were in full swing. My brother, dressed in his finest clothes and adorned with garlands, sat in an ornate throne-like chair. We had decorated the background really nicely. My brother greeted the male guests with the customary alai-balai, embracing them first on the left side and then on the right. As darkness fell, the bride's family and relatives began to arrive. The invited guests handed over their gifts of ten or twenty rupees to my brother and sat down to eat. Our wedding dinners are a grand affair. We are not rich, but when it comes to wedding dinners, we are no less than royalty. We arranged the tables, covered them with the dastar cloth and laid out porcelain plates in which we served bagara rice. In a side plate, mutton curry was placed along with dalcha, a special type of lentil soup cooked with bottle gourd. Then there was curd chutney. We refilled the bowls and plates as soon as they got empty. At long last, the final course, the sweet dish of double ka meetha was served individually to every guest. As soon as one group of guests finished their meal, we ran up, dusted the table cloths and readied the tables for the next round of guests.

Muslim dinners and parties are known for their sumptuous and delicious fare. So there was a huge rush with everyone in the village, even those not invited, turning up for the feast. We were slogging nonstop, and yet the number of guests waiting to eat seemed never-ending! Parashuram and I were prompt and quick in serving the food, but Narendar, not used to such work, was rather slow. Parashuram and I had to take the help of three or four young male relatives in serving. My other friends in the village did not offer to help as they were not so close to my family and were unfamiliar with my relatives.

Even before half of the guests had eaten, we realised that the bagara rice wouldn't suffice. Oh my god, how we panicked! All my uncles, maternal and paternal, hurriedly got together and cooked some more rice. Just then, the groom was brought to the dining table. He was accompanied by his brothers-in-law and several male members of the bride's family who make it a point to sit down to eat with the groom, because they know they would get to eat the best and juiciest pieces of mutton. For our part, we served the meat liberally because after all, they were the bride's family and relatives. We kept refilling their plates with meat and they kept eating. All of them gobbled up the meat, but they hadn't even touched the lentil dalcha. Only the discerning few who knew that dalcha was no ordinary dish ate it and said that it had turned out well. We filled up four plates with the desert and placed them before the bride's party so they could help themselves to their heart's content.

By the time the men had finished eating, it was ten. All the youngsters helping us slipped away one by one, leaving only Parashuram and me to serve. After the last male guest had eaten, we went outside for a break. We drew up chairs and sat next to my brother to rest a while. Narendar had already eaten as he was forced to sit down along with my brother for dinner. Neither Parashuram nor I, nor any of my family members was in the mood to eat.

After the men, the women were invited to eat. Our women folk—cousins, sisters and aunts—began to serve the women guests as they sat down to eat. By then, the bagara rice was over and they only got plain rice to eat. Even the mutton curry was nearly over. Only the first batch of women, those on the bride's side, got to eat the curry. Those who sat in the next round got none.

By the time all the women had eaten, there were three rounds, it was midnight. It was only then that Parashuram and I were asked to eat. There were ten of us in all who had not eaten. But we did not feel like eating; we were too exhausted even for hunger. After serving food to so many people, the very sight and smell of food puts one off. Besides, everyone else was too tired to serve us. So Narendar said, 'Come and eat, I will serve you.' He brought us whatever food remained—only plain rice and dalcha. There was no meat, not even curd chutney. We managed to finish our meal with a bit of the leftover bagara baigan curry. As for the double ka meetha, we didn't even get a morsel.

We had barely rested for two days before the wedding in Narendar's house was upon us. Once again, it was the same kind of frenzied activity and bustle. We took care of all the 'outside' work that needed to be done. Since Narendar was the only son in the family, we were even more deeply involved in the wedding preparations. Although the family had several relatives in the village, none of them came forward to help. They are all used to being served, but not sharing work. Narendar's family belonged to the reddy community and had once been well off. But excessive largesse led to their present impoverished condition. There were only three reddy households in the entire village. And this was the first reddy wedding in a long time; therefore none of us was aware of reddy marriage customs. As a result, we had to go round and round in circles trying to get even the smallest of things done.

The night before the wedding, we began to decorate the house. As I cut out designs from different coloured paper, my friends stuck them all over the house, giving it a festive look. After slogging for hours, we barely got a few winks of sleep when we were woken up and then it began all over again, rushing here and there, in and out of the house, trying to get every last thing done in time.

Finally, the groom's party arrived. As they entered the village, we received them with booming drums. The guests were ushered into the house to the rhythmic beats of the drums. As the auspicious hour of the marriage approached, a new problem reared its head. The brahmin priest who would conduct the nuptial ceremony was nowhere to be seen. One of us borrowed a guest's bike and went in search of the priest in the neighbouring village. He had agreed to perform two other weddings on the same day. So the wedding that was to take place at 9.46 am was finally performed only around mid-noon!

The moment the bride and groom became wife and husband, the guests were invited to partake of lunch. Everyone was eager to eat, but no one came forward to serve. Once again, the task fell upon Parashuram and me. We rolled out mats for the guests to sit on. Then we kept leaf plates made of dry almond leaves in front of the mats in long rows. As Parashuram began to serve steaming hot rice from a large bowl, I followed him with a bucket full of curry, serving it with a ladle onto the leaf plates. Parashuram, as I have mentioned before, is extremely quick. And he also kept up a friendly banter with each guest as he served them. 'Greetings, Anna! Is the serving enough? Thatha, namasthe! Some more rice for you? Please have some more, Kakkayya?' he would say. And I would be amazed at the ease, familiarity and speed with which he served. Before I had served curry to even half the seated guests, Parashuram had already finished serving rice to everyone! He stood there with his bowl of rice, urging me to serve faster. 'Don't be so slow, Baba!' he called out to me with a laugh. Parashuram had a word for everyone; he laughed and joked and went from person to person to see if they wanted more helpings of rice. I stood in the middle with my buckets of curry and lentil soup, alert to requests for more. Other men filled the glasses with water and refilled them again and again.

The Communist Party of India had come to the village in our own time. In fact, Narendar was one of the youngsters responsible for setting up a unit of the party in Keshurajupally. At Narendar's behest, Parashuram had also joined the party. But our Muslim families were all supporters of the Indian National Congress. Caught between family and friends, I chose to remain independent. Naturally, all our communist friends had turned up for the wedding.

Just then I heard Parashuram call me. The first round of guests had finished eating and were getting up to wash their hands. I looked around for chakali Pullaiah to clear up the used leaf plates. But he was nowhere to be seen. So the task of cleaning up, too, fell upon the two of us. We picked up the leaf plates, rolling them up one by one, and dumped them into the large dustbin kept outside. Just then Pullaiah turned up looking apologetic. 'Sir, why are you taking the trouble when I am here?' he protested and picked up a broom to sweep away the rice and the bones picked clean by the guests and heaped on the sides of the plates. Once the place was cleaned up, Parashuram and I picked up a fresh bunch of leaf plates to serve the next round of guests. Even as we stood with the plates in hand, I heard a commotion in the neighbouring room. An old man was shouting. Everyone was crowding into the room. Some of them began to speak in whispers, looking around furtively. I was puzzled. I pushed my way in through the crowd to see what was happening. I heard a man shouting about something. Some people tried to pacify him, but he would not listen. He seemed to have found support among several others in the room. I tried to move in further and craned my neck to get a better view.

Just then Narendar's father entered the room. He went up to the old man. 'What is it? What is going on here?' he asked anxiously.

'How dare you do this to us! What do you think of us? Are you not born a reddy? How dare you get a madiga to serve us food!' the old man screamed in rage.

My head reeled as his words hit me. Some leaf plates slipped from my hands. I felt an electric shock run through my body, because we never hear such things in our Muslim households when we are all seated around the dastar to eat. I turned around quickly to see where Parashuram was. I was worried he might have heard those words which were sure to have hurt him grievously. But there was no sign of him. Parashuram had already left. Only the leaf plates were lying on the ground where he had been standing.

Translated by **R. Akhileshwari**

9

Sheer Khorma

It was Ramzan. Jani was walking towards the idgah. He was in a hurry now. By the time he had bought the milk and all the other things that ammi wanted for Ramzan, it had got late. Salma's beautiful face—the face that brought tranquillity to his mind—flashed before his eyes. His heart began to race. As soon as the namaz is over I shall first go to Salma's house, he told himself and quickened his pace.

The idgah was at the western end of the town. The Ramzan and Bakrid prayers were always held there. But it lay half a mile outside town. The town was fairly large, about the size of a taluq. Dust rose from the road with all the scooters and motorcycles speeding by. There were a lot of people walking on the road along with him. Everyone was dressed in new clothes. The different colourful caps on their heads and the fragrance of perfumes they wore made the road look like a floating flower garden. The older ones had tied kerchiefs over their heads. Some had even brought their little grandchildren along.

They could now hear Imam Sahib adjusting the mike at the idgah. Jani walked faster. He carried a plastic bag in his hand. It contained an old blanket and a satin cap that ammi had taken out of the trunk for him. He was wearing clothes he had ironed and kept ready the night before, and a pair of worn out hawai chappals on his feet. He was nearing the idgah. On either side of the path sat fakirs, pleading for alms. A couple of them sang qawwalis to the accompaniment of the marfa and kanjeera. Many people sat alongside the newly built compound wall of the idgah, calling out to the arriving visitors to leave their footwear with them. They were all competing with each other to attract the highest number. Jani stood undecided for a few seconds, wondering where to leave his slippers. Then he noticed a gentle looking old man sitting in front of him. He removed his slippers, shoved one into the other and handed them to the old man, who kept them along with the pile of footwear he was minding. As more and more people made their way in, Jani moved towards the entrance of the idgah. Imam Sahib began,

Avuz Billahi Minshaithan Nir-rahim
Bismillah Hir-rahman Nir-rahim
I seek God's protection from the Devil
I begin by invoking the name of the All Merciful God

Everyone was now in a terrible rush to get inside. Jani pushed himself in along with the crowd. Some were grumbling that the entrance ought to have been built wider. He saw the idgah masjid at the far end. In front of it was a huge neem tree. Jani hurried towards it. There were many who had already occupied the space under the shade of the tree. He looked everywhere but realised it was futile to look for a shaded spot. So he took out his blanket and spread it out in one corner, and three others promptly sat down beside him when they saw there was extra space.

The sun was sharp. Jani glanced at the watch on the wrist of the man beside him. It was past eleven. Had he come earlier, he would have found a space in the shade. He looked back—there were more and still more people pouring in. They were hurriedly spreading their sheets and sitting down wherever they could. Those without sheets would stand and wait until they found a spot on someone else's sheet. Some just sat on the bare ground. Many were sweating in the heat. Many had worn new clothes, but there were also those who hadn't and they looked less enthused and somewhat downcast. Some faces were full of worry. Some faces looked more mature than their years, more wrinkled than was natural, their eyes sunken, sleep-deprived and lifeless. Allah! They say that all these are tests that You put us through. Why do You subject so many to such misery?!

Imam Sahib continued to deliver his bayan. Time moved on. The incoming crowds gradually thinned down. Imam Sahib ended his speech and began to expound on the mode of prayer for the festival. In a few minutes the entire assembled jamat stood up for namaz. The men stood shoulder to shoulder and began to form rows. As the rows were being formed, those behind quickly moved forward to fill in the gaps in the front rows. Allah-o-Akbar! Imam Sahib raised his hands and began the prayer.

When the namaz ended, before beginning the dua, Imam Sahib gave a lecture on takhreer, the conduct appropriate for a Muslim. But Jani was not listening. He sat there lost in his own thoughts. No new clothes for him this year. With the money he had managed to save from time to time, he had bought a sari for his mother. She was saddened. 'Why did you buy for me, beta? You should have bought a readymade shirt or trousers for yourself instead!' she had said. 'It's all right, Ammi. It's hardly been six months since I got a new pair.' She had pleaded with him to return the sari and get something for himself. But he did not listen to her.

Imam Sahib began the dua, prayers for mercy. All assembled extended their arms in prayer. Jani looked at his hands. Oil-stained hands. Stains that refused to go away, just like the stubborn stains of poverty. Stains that stuck to his fingertips even after he trimmed his nails and washed his hands, just like his persistent, unrelenting melancholy.

In his prayers, Imam Sahib pleaded with Allah that all human beings should prosper, that there should be plentiful rains, that there should be no famine—he pleaded for all kinds of good things for everyone. To all of these, Jani kept saying, Ameen, along with all the others. But in his mind, all he could see was his mother's sorrowful eyes, his younger sister's frightened face, and his elder sister's anxiety. Tears sprang to his eyes. Will he ever be able to fill their lives with some joy? Allah! Won't You come to our rescue? Allah! Won't You grant us some happiness?

Salma ... How wonderful it would be if he could marry Salma by next Ramzan! Allah, grant me that one thing, if nothing else. After the dua, everyone got to their feet and embraced each other, exchanging Id greetings. Jani scanned the faces in the crowd to see if there was someone he knew, but he couldn't find a single familiar face. Just then, the old grandpa who had shared his blanket stretched out his arms and wished him, 'Id Mubarak, beta!' Jani's heart filled with joy. 'May God keep you safe, Chacha!' he greeted and embraced the old man wholeheartedly. He was reminded of the saying that those who have no one else in the world have God. He picked up his blanket, folded it and put it back into the bag. On his way out, he met a few distant relatives and a couple of his neighbours. He greeted and embraced all of them before walking towards the idgah gate. As he scanned the crowds again, he wondered why he hadn't met any of his uncles. Everyone was now in a great hurry to leave. It took quite a while to get out. At the spot where he had left his slippers, there was a huge scramble as people were pushing and jostling each other to grab their footwear and leave. They gave the old man minding the slippers a rupee or two as they collected their pair. Jani looked for his slippers, spotted them in a corner and put them on. The old man was worried that people might slip away without paying him and he held out his hand and looked at everyone anxiously. Jani managed to put two rupees into his hand with some difficulty because of the milling crowd. As he was moving away, a strong foot fell between his slipper and his raised right foot. He nearly fell but managed to steady himself. He looked down at his slipper. His heart sank. It had broken from the heel upwards. It was already a little broken to begin with. He lifted his foot—the half-broken slipper dangled from it. He took it off and examined it. There was nothing to be done; only the very end of the slipper still held together, the rest had fallen apart.

The old man looked at Jani and the broken slipper and said, 'Oh! That is unfortunate, son.'

Jani suddenly felt like bursting into tears but he collected himself and threw the broken slippers aside in anger. Though he had been sitting in the sun all this while, he didn't perspire. But now that he had lost his slippers, he broke into a sweat and his kurta was soon soaked.

'They are just old chappals, beta. Just think that you have gotten rid of all your ill luck along with them! Buy yourself a new pair and you will fare well,' the old man consoled Jani.

Sigh. Yes, they were just old chappals. But he didn't have the money to buy a new pair. And he had planned to go to Salma's after the namaz. Now what was he to do? How could he go to their house without any footwear? Jani stood there for a long time, watching everyone leave. The old man also left. Jani felt bleak and empty. He slowly began to walk out. 'Ayya! Ayya! Sir! Baba!' the fakirs called out, their voices mingling with the sounds of the marfa and the clanging of the kanjeera. People moved along, donating alms to the fakirs. Jani didn't have small change even for that. He walked for some distance. On his left was the graveyard. There were several people standing before their elders' graves, showering flowers and offering prayers. Jani moved towards his father's grave. Flowers were being sold outside the graveyard, but he had no money for flowers either. He walked through the tombstones, trying to avoid the thorny bushes and stones. He stood in front of his father's grave. His grandparents' graves lay next to his father's. The person standing in front of a grave nearby carefully unwrapped the flowers he was carrying in a leaf and showered them upon the grave. He then proceeded to shower the remaining flowers on the surrounding graves. He also offered them to Jani. Jani murmured his thanks as he took a few and sprinkled the petals upon his father's grave and on the ones next to it. He stood there and offered a prayer.

Memories of his father flooded his mind. If only abba were alive, we wouldn't have to face so many troubles. He came out of the graveyard and stood there, wondering what to do. He didn't feel like going to Salma's house anymore. His heart was full of sorrow. How could he visit any of his relatives with bare feet? He slowly began the long walk homewards. All of that morning's enthusiasm had evaporated. But his mind was filled with Salma. He passed by her lane. He felt a terrible rage against someone, he didn't know who, because he couldn't visit her. At last he reached his house. He pushed aside the cloth curtain and stepped inside.

Gori Ma was busy making bagara rice. 'Salam alaikum, Ammi,' he wished his mother and touched her feet. She blessed him, praying that he should live a hundred years and that he should get married by the next Ramzan. Then she asked him, 'You didn't go to visit anyone? How come you are back so early?' Jani wearily flopped onto the bed. Gori Ma asked him, 'What is wrong, beta? Why do you look so downcast?' He lay down on the cot and said, 'Nothing'. 'There will soon be a stream of relatives visiting. I better finish the cooking,' she said and hurried back to her work.

Jani's mind was filled with the image of Salma's beautiful face. He was restless. He *really* wanted to see her. What a beautiful smile she had! Her smile could make him forget all his woes. She must be waiting for me. I should go meet her. Today was a festival day and a perfect excuse to visit her. On other days, it would be difficult and awkward to go there. But how? Perhaps ammi has some money ...

'Ammi, my chappal broke when I was at the idgah today,' he said finally.

'Ayyo! How did that happen?'

'Someone stepped on it in the crowd and it broke.'

'Curse this misery! Never mind. You can buy new ones. I have fifteen rupees with me. I've been saving it for a long time. But will fifteen be enough to buy a new pair?'

Just then they heard a sound outside the door and Jani quickly got up and drew the curtains aside to see who it was. Ammi's brother, Chand Mama had come. Jani greeted him, 'Salam alaikum, Mamu!'

'Valaikum salam, Jani! You didn't come to the idgah?' his uncle asked as they embraced each other in the alai-balai way. Jani replied, 'I did, Mamu! I was also looking for you!'

Chand Mama bent down and touched Gori Ma's feet as he greeted her, 'Salam alaikum, Apa!' She blessed him. He sat for a while, ate the sheer khorma that ammi had prepared for the festival, and while leaving, pressed a fifty rupee note into her palm. As soon as he left, Gori Ma gave the money to Jani, asking him to buy new footwear. He was overjoyed! As he stepped out of the house, he saw his younger uncle, and his friend Kakkayya approaching from opposite sides. He greeted and embraced each of them in turn and set off to meet Salma. He stopped on the way to buy slippers, ordinary ones that cost him thirty rupees. Jani could barely wait to see her.

Salma was the daughter of his eldest uncle. Their house lay on the other end of town. And since it was far, mutual visits were infrequent. But occasionally, he did go to meet her. Everyone in her family liked him. They always said, 'Jani is a very good lad'.

Jani's family's troubles had begun with the death of his father. His mother had struggled to get both his sisters married. Jani had managed to study only up to the eighth standard. As the debts from his sisters' marriages kept mounting, it became really difficult to make ends meet at home. Ultimately, Gori Ma was forced to seek work for Jani in a tractor mechanic shed. She thought it would teach him some useful skills and also help to keep their household running. So Jani left for work every day at eight in the morning and there was no telling when he would return at night. Gori Ma was alone at home the whole day. She began to pester him to get married so she would have a daughter-in-law for company. He wanted to marry Salma. He had mentioned this to his mother.

Gori Ma had said, 'Beta, you are the kind who never asks for anything. This is the only thing you have ever asked for. I will do all I can. I have been thinking of the girl myself. I don't see who else your uncle will want to get her married to. Let us wait for the right time, and I will broach the subject.'

The next time Jani had gone to Salma's house, he had somehow found the courage to ask her, 'Salma, do you like me?' She had lowered her gaze shyly, nodded as if to say yes and run into the next room. This had only made him more restless with desire. This year he was determined to marry her.

Now he stood outside Salma's door and knocked. He hoped she would come to open the door. But her brother Haneef opened it. 'Salam alaikum, bhai jaan!' Haneef wished him. 'Valaikum salam!' he replied as he embraced Haneef, and walked in. His aunt was in the living room. He offered her his salam. She greeted him in return and asked, 'Come, Jani. How is your mother?'

'She is well, Mami. She sends you her greetings. Hasn't Mamu returned from the idgah yet?'

'He has. He has gone to Rahmat Nagar to visit a distant cousin of mine.'

Jani thought, Ah. So he went to visit a distant cousin before he visited us!

'Please sit, Jani. I'll get you some sheer khorma,' his aunt said and disappeared into the kitchen.

Jani sat down in a chair. His eyes searched for Salma. Where was the Salma who would run out as soon as she heard him arrive, whose eyes and face would light up on seeing him? He knew that Salma's room was on the left side of the living room in which he now sat. There was a curtain hanging in the entrance to that room. Why didn't she come out to see him? Had she gone to visit her friends? But she knew he would come; she wouldn't have gone. Jani wondered what was going on. He called Haneef and whispered, 'Where is Salma?' Haneef gestured towards the room, 'Inside.' He wanted to ask him to call her out. But just then his aunt came in with a bowl of sheer khorma and handed it to him. Jani took the bowl from her.

It was Salma who always served him the sheer khorma, whether it was Ramzan or Bakrid. She would come to him wearing shiny new clothes, a long voni, and her radiant, smiling face. Having her come and stand so close to him and breathing in her sweet fragrance was enough to fill him with a pleasurable lightness. Eating the sheer khorma was like tasting nectar. She would withdraw to stand at a little distance and politely enquire after his mother and sisters with an entranced gaze fixed on him all the while. As for himself, he wouldn't take his eyes off her face for a moment and respond to each of her queries with a boundless joy suffusing him. Their eyes spoke a wordless, silent language. Today, Jani felt awkward and uneasy that he had to eat the khorma without seeing Salma. Mami was asking him about this and that and he managed to answer her half-heartedly as he swallowed a spoonful. He didn't want to eat any more. He didn't know what to do. He kept glancing in the direction of Salma's room as he sat holding the bowl. He couldn't understand why Salma didn't come out. If any other Id visitors arrived now, he will have no chance of meeting her at all! What to do? He was anxious and confused.

Meanwhile, his aunt was thinking, Why doesn't the boy finish his sheer khorma quickly and leave! Why is he just sitting there? I have so much work to do! Then she noticed Jani glancing repeatedly at Salma's room. She understood and shifted uncomfortably. She couldn't wait any longer and came out with the truth.

'Why don't you have the sheer khorma, beta?' she began. Jani was flustered. He began to eat. 'I mentioned my distant cousin, didn't I? Their son lives in Saudi. He is here on a two-month leave. His parents want to get him married. They asked for our Salma. They said, "She is such a pretty girl, we don't want any dowry". They just want a grand wedding. The boy is a nice fellow, he is educated, and works in Saudi. So your uncle agreed immediately. We have to conduct the nikah in just a month's time! I hope you don't mind, beta, but we couldn't inform you earlier. It all happened so quickly you see. Your uncle will come and inform your mother. He might come to visit you today itself. We all want our daughters to live a comfortable life, free of all troubles, don't we, beta? Moreover, these days who will want to marry without a fat dowry? And you know that your uncle can't afford much ...' She went on and on, carried away with the joy and relief of having found such a good match for her daughter.

Jani suddenly felt as if he couldn't breathe. Nothing she said after this entered his head. Salma's wedding was fixed with someone else. She would go away to Saudi. He would never see her again. His head swirled. The sheer khorma tasted bitter. Sharp hot tears stung his eyes. He abruptly put the bowl down on the table, got up and walked out of the house without looking back. Mami was upset and called out, 'Jani beta, what happened? Why are you leaving like this?'

Jani stepped out of the house and stood on the road. A great blackness engulfed him. He sobbed out aloud, his sobs nearly choking him. He began to walk briskly, not knowing where he was headed.

Translated by **Uma Maheswari Bhrugubanda**

10

Life in Death

I woke up first. Shaheen was still fast asleep next to me. Like me she too must have struggled to get some sleep last night. I mustn't disturb her. I got up and stepped out of bed as softly as I could. How very light my feet felt! Something wasn't right. I looked back at the bed. How strange—there I was, still lying on it! A cold shiver ran through my body. No, not quite. Because my body was not with me. I didn't understand what was going on. My brain went numb. No, that wasn't possible either. Because even that was not with me! I was utterly confused. Have I ...? No ... Have I *died?* No! No! That could never happen. I mustn't let that happen. I quickly stepped back and lay down precisely where my body was on the bed. When I moved my limbs, they felt weightless like feathers! But when I looked down on the bed, my hands and legs lay heavy and stiff like logs. I couldn't move them an inch. Now I was truly scared. But could I really *feel* scared? There was pain, though. This meant that I was dead. Tch-tch. I have died. Actually died. Okay so that was it then. It felt like someone was twisting a knife in my heart—the sensation was that painful. My god, how many tasks had I left unfinished! And here I was, dead already. Not completed even forty years of my life. Why did this happen to me so soon? Chhah!

Quite recently, I did contemplate death. I had thought that it might befall me quite suddenly before I was prepared for it. And I thought I must do everything I wanted to do in this life before that happened. But now it has happened. I *have* died. I, Yousuf, am dead. What do I do now? I sat up. I looked down—my body was still in a horizontal position. My face looked peaceful enough, and serene, as if I was asleep without a care. I looked at my face as if for the very first time. It had never looked like this all those times that I have looked at it in the mirror. I was overwhelmed by sadness. I gently took my face into my two hands. Despite all the wrinkles, how adorable it looked! It was astonishing how I had managed to swim through the sea of troubles and strife and misery that had flooded these past forty years. It is true there were people who thoroughly disliked me. But then there were also many who loved me—perhaps the only thing I could be content about.

I bent forward and kissed my forehead. I felt two teardrops fall. But for tears to fall, there must be eyes—my eyes were still closed, I could see them. Oh the copious tears these eyes had shed! The rage and agony they had reflected! The irreverent laughter that had danced in these eyes. The many worlds they had glimpsed! Now these eyes are shut forever.

But the question is what should I do now? Should I wake up my begum? Won't she be terribly upset? Will she be able to bear the news of my death? What about my children? How innocent they looked asleep! If they come to know that I am dead, they would surely cry their little hearts out. How will these people live without me? How will they carry on? What a terrible thing to happen and so suddenly. The other day when I felt a peculiar and sharp pain in my left arm, I fervently hoped it was not going to be a heart attack. Of course, Shaheen pestered me into going for a medical check-up. The tests showed that I had high blood pressure. The doctor said there were some changes in the way my heart was beating. I didn't pay much attention. Have I now died of a heart attack? I don't think so. Have I really and truly died, or am I just imagining it? Let me try to move my body. Uff! It doesn't budge an inch! I shoved it hard. No. It's no use. I cannot move it at all. It is like stone.

Once this news reaches my village, my parents will go into shock; my sisters will have a heart attack. And my younger brother, he certainly won't be able to take it. Poor Shaheen! She had been so worried about my health. Of late, she had been urging me to get home early. She would constantly inquire if I was feeling tired or uneasy or unwell. She probably had her own doubts about my health. But what's the use? After all the care she took of me, I have died. And there is nothing anyone can do to change it now. Every time I phoned my mother, she would say, 'Take care of your health, beta.' Oh why did I never pay any attention to her!

Ah! Looks like Shaheen just woke up. She opened her eyes and looked at me, that is, at my body. She doesn't know that I am dead. Oh how I wish she would call me or shake me awake. Maybe she will do that now. I better get back into my body and lie down. I lay down and turned to her side. Shaheen got up from bed. Dearest Shaheen, I think I am dead. Will you please call out my name? Will you please just wake me up? But she went out of the room. Shaheen! SHAHEEN! I called as loud as I could. It's no use. She cannot hear me. I felt angry, miserable, helpless.

I too got up and walked out of the room. Shaheen went into the bathroom. I looked into our bedroom. I could see my body still lying where I lay earlier. But then how is it that I am standing here? I tried to look at my standing self—Nothing. I could see nothing. A huge cold rock settled into my heart when I realised that I, this *I*, had no connection with my body anymore. Worse, I had no connection with this world anymore. But that is only to be expected when you die. How precarious, how fragile life is. And all the while we are only concerned about our property, our money, our house, our relatives ... What a waste!

The house filled with the typical sounds of morning. Sunlight was pouring in. Shaheen came out of the bathroom and went past me into our bedroom. She could not see me standing here. Will she wake me up? No, she won't do that. She always waits for me to wake up by myself because she knows I have insomnia. She had put on her chunni and come out. I kept muttering, Shaheen, please try and wake me up ... please. I went towards her but she walked right through me! Sigh. It's no use. I just followed her. Shaheen went to wake up our two children, calling them out by name. Nasreen has to go to school and Suleiman, to college. Normally, by now one of them is up and about. But today neither of them had woken up. Perhaps they were up watching TV late into the night. Hearing their mother call, they got up. I looked into our bedroom again hopefully, thinking that perhaps I too would be able to wake up—no luck.

The children got busy with their morning ablutions and getting ready, and Shaheen got busy preparing their lunch boxes. No one paid any attention to me. On a normal day, I would tell them not to bother me. But today, I dearly wished someone would come and wake me up. What should I do now? Should I just keep lying like this until someone came to my body? Anyhow, it seemed better to lie inside my body. My mind was teaming with thoughts of what was going to happen in this house once they finally realise that I am dead. Relatives, personal friends and political friends from the Marxist-Leninist movement will come. But it will not be possible to keep my body in this rented house. They will have to take the body to our own house in the village, a hundred kilometres away. But most of my friends are in Hyderabad. What then?

There was not a single paisa in our house. I was not the kind who would think about tomorrow. And now I have gone and died so suddenly. Will Shaheen be able manage this house alone? Will the children be able complete their studies? Shaheen would often tell me, 'It is not enough to think about society alone. Please also think about our future, my future, our children's future ...' What she had feared most has now happened.

I felt like smoking a cigarette. Let me light one as I do my thinking. I got up and reached for the pack of cigarettes lying close by. Strange. I couldn't pick it up. It wouldn't come into my hand. My fingers went right through it! Hah! Yousuf, you can't even smoke a cigarette. Death to you! But of course, you are already dead.

'Abba jaan! Abba jaan!' Suleiman was calling me as he walked into our bedroom. I couldn't get up. I continued to lie still. I was so confused. Should I or should I not get up? Will my body rise along with me? What if it doesn't? Let me see what he does.

Suleiman came and shook my body. I was overjoyed! Any moment now I would open my eyes sleepily and say, What is it, beta? And I would sit up. I watched myself anxiously. No. My body was like a log. Lifeless. It moved this way and that as my son shook it. But it did not move on its own, nor did it sit up. No. It was all over. Suleiman seemed surprised and he kept shaking my body and calling me, 'Abba jaan ... Abba jaan!' his voice now rising in anxiety. But my body wouldn't respond. It was now confirmed. I have indeed left this world. An unbearable bottomless melancholy engulfed me.

Suleiman screamed, 'Ammi! Ammi! Come quickly!' He knew.

'Kya hua beta? What happened?' Shaheen came running into our room, with my daughter Nasreen close behind her.

My wife and my children were holding on to each other and crying out aloud. It was so difficult to watch them cry. I too felt like crying. I didn't know what to do. I wanted so much to console them, but what was the use. They couldn't see me or hear me. All they could see was my dead body. The house soon began to fill up with neighbours.

'Poor man. I believe he died of a heart attack.'

'He was perfectly fine when he spoke to me last night. How come he died so suddenly?'

'Does death ever announce itself?'

'He was a good man ...'

'It's always the good people who go to God soon.'

'Every Sunday he would be attending some meeting or the other. He never stayed at home.'

'Ayyo, poor fellow!'

I could hear all this, but my mind was focused on how to console my wife and children. Women from our neighbourhood were trying to comfort Shaheen.

'Of late, I felt he wasn't as active as he used to be. But I never dreamed he would go like this. My children and I have been orphaned. Allah, why? Why have You done this to us! Isn't this a grave injustice ...?' Shaheen wailed in between her sobs. My son and my daughter were inconsolable.

People received the news over the phone. Close friends from Hyderabad, family friends, and those associated with the movement I was involved in—everyone came. Even those who had moved away from me due to ideological differences. How I wished I could talk to them! I was surprised to see my old friend Saidulu. I thought he may not have received the news, and that even if he did, he would not come. We had not been in touch for over a year. Seeing him, I longed for an alai-balai embrace from him. Saidulu stood next to my dead body and started crying. After a while he regained his composure and consoled Shaheen and the children. He assured them he would always be there to help them. Then he came out of the house and began to supervise all arrangements to take my body to Nalgonda. He hired a vehicle to carry my body, and everyone followed the vehicle. Other friends hired another vehicle to come to my village for the funeral. The van set out from Hyderabad towards Nalgonda. My body was covered with a bedsheet. On one side sat my wife and children and on the other side sat Saidulu; next to him was my son's friend, a colleague from work and a friend from the CPI (ML-Maoist) Party. Saidulu covered his face with a handkerchief to hide his tears.

Saidulu and I had been close right from childhood days. It was only in the past one year that we had not been on talking terms. Before that, we would meet at least once every two or three weeks and have a good time together. Sometime back, Saidulu needed to borrow fifty thousand rupees from a finance company to pay off some loans. He asked me to sign as a guarantor, and I did so without hesitation. But he couldn't pay them back; so I became responsible for paying that money. Shaheen was so upset that she had a minor squabble with him over this matter, and that spoiled the relationship between Saidulu and me. We have not spoken to each other or met for over a year now. Of course, the growing traffic woes of Hyderabad also did not help. He lived in one corner of the city, and I in another. Meeting each other became a chore, and indeed, we also lost interest in trying to meet. What a pity that it is my death that has brought us together today. I kept thinking about Saidulu, my other childhood friends and acquaintances from my office. I wondered if all of them had heard the news yet. My son's cell phone rang every now and then. Suleiman was now carrying my cell phone as well; he was finding it difficult to inform every caller about my death.

We reached Nalgonda. The entire street near my house stood waiting. The moment the van stopped, many of them began to wail. I kept looking for my mother; she could no longer walk without support. Someone helped her walk up to the van. As she saw my body, she screamed, 'Beta! ... Yousuf beta!' and she slumped in a faint. I flew to her and entwined her in a tight hug, but she saw and felt nothing. Suleiman jumped down from the van and caught my mother in his arms. My sisters held my little Nasreen and tried to console her. What a terrible and heart-wrenching scene it was! They lifted my body down from the vehicle and kept it on the cot in front of my parents' house, pushing aside people who kept gathering all the while. The sound of loud weeping and wailing reached the heavens. Someone removed the sheet from my face. My mother and sisters collapsed in a heap on top of my body. My younger brother wept as he beat his chest. My father came up to my body, tears streaming down his face, cupped my face in his hands and said, 'My son! How could you leave this world before us, my son?' My mother was slapping her head with her hands and repeating, 'How will we cope with this loss? I never thought I would live to witness this.'

I was watching all this and thinking, what had I ever done to help these people, except perhaps utter some kind words that may have soothed them on occasion. In some cases, my words did not make any sense to them and some of my deeds may have even hurt them. So how is it that they love me so much? I should have taken better care of my health, and of them. But what to do! I was never the kind to do so. Shaheen used to say, 'You think more about others than your own kith and kin.' Who is one's own and who are others? Today, I have lost connection with one and all. Tomorrow, I will be dust.

Midday already. They wanted to bury me ahead of the magrib namaz before the sun sets. They asked for the qabr to be prepared. They boiled water with neem leaves to give my body the final ritual bath. Saidulu was overseeing everything. The house was filled with relatives. The shock and grief had left my family completely drained. My friends from Hyderabad had arrived; all of them looked terribly upset. My body was moved onto a wooden plank kept in the front yard of my house. People stood around, holding a sheet over my body by the four sides. Of the two strangers I did not recognise, one with a beard covered my body with a white sheet and removed all the clothes I was wearing. With my brother standing near my head and my son towards my legs, he started scrubbing my body with a piece of soap. They poured a lot of water and gave me a nice long bath. In fact I don't think I have had a bath like that since childhood when my mother used to bathe me! But this was truly my last one. After the bath, they wiped my body thoroughly, wrapped it in a white sheet and lay me down on the wooden plank. Only my face was visible. Everyone was asked to take a final glimpse of my body before it was taken away. People began to move past me in a line. My mother, my sisters and my daughter were towards the end of the line. As they came closer, their sobs grew louder.

At last it was my mother's turn. Ammi, who was only half-conscious, was made to sit down on a chair next to my body. Someone urged her, 'Doodh baksho!' In a weak voice, she uttered these words with difficulty: 'Doodh bakshti hoon. As a mother, I set you free from the debt of milk you owe me. I give up all my maternal rights over you, beta,' and broke down.

I could do nothing for this woman who gave me birth. I never really cared for her ... Chhah! What kind of a useless life have I led!

Shaheen came next, led by the women from our neighbourhood. She fell over my body and started sobbing uncontrollably even as elders asked her to restrain herself. Someone shouted, 'Offer the mehr! Offer the mehr!' Another voice said, 'Two tolas of silver, one tola of gold, plus twenty-five thousand rupees.' Shaheen quietly repeated these words and added, 'Mehr bakshti hoon. I give up my right to the gift of mehr owed to me at marriage.'

What a miserable, pathetic life I have led. I couldn't even pay back such a small amount of mehr to my own Shaheen.

'Come on, let us go,' someone urged. They covered my face and my entire body with cloth and bound it with ropes. The wails and desolate cries of my family could be heard especially when they lifted my body. My daughter wouldn't let go of my lifeless body and clung to it. Someone gently pulled her aside. They brought my body outside the house, lifted it into the casket and covered it with a green cloth. As the cries and wails reached a crescendo, they lifted the casket. 'La Ilaha Illallah, Mohammadur Rasoolillah,' they chanted as they shifted the casket from one shoulder to another and the funeral procession began to move towards the burial ground. On the way, passersby also came forward to carry my body for a while.

We reached the masjid. After the janaza namaz was read at the masjid, the journey continued. We entered the burial ground where a pit had been dug. They put down the casket and removed the cloth covering it. One person descended into the pit, sprayed attar and rosewater in it. Everyone was asked to take a look at my face for the last time. I, too, looked at my face ... I might never get to see it again. My friend Saidulu came running to see my face for the last time—he had traveled nearly three hundred kilometres just for this. Seeing all these people and relatives who took the trouble of coming to take a last look at my dead face, I thought they were so much more loving and generous than I had ever been. My brother and my son wiped their tears. My son, my uncles and nephews all held the casket and lowered it into the grave with ropes. One more person got into the grave and pushed the body to one side to arrange the stones to hold the casket in place. After he had climbed out, everyone picked up lumps of fresh mud and began to throw them in.

I felt the mud hit and splatter all over my face and body. I sat up feeling utterly disoriented and bewildered. Shaheen was still asleep next to me. I was in Hyderabad in our rented house. And I was sitting up in my own bed. This means I am *not* dead! I gingerly touched my face, my neck, arms, legs—I was *alive*! My heart was beating regularly. I could clearly feel my pulse. Oh God, what a relief! Had I died, I would have caused such a lot of trouble to everyone. Now I must work hard and fast to lessen their burdens. I must also work for the betterment of society; there is so much that needs to be done. And I must take care of my health. But first of all I must call all these people who care so much about me. What an age we live in. Running like mad all the time. And for what? It is taking us away from the very people who care most about us. It is ages since I spoke to any of them even on phone. It has been a whole year since I spoke to Saidulu. How could a mere fifty thousand rupees have come between us?

I picked up my mobile phone and called Saidulu.

Translated by **D. Vasanta**

11

Nowhere to Turn

Osman shut down his shop and started walking home. The lanes were dark. Dogs and pigs were roaming about. Carefully avoiding them, he entered the narrow inner galli, picking his way over the pavement made of cemented shahbad stones. The lane felt congested, just like his mind. On one side there was an open drain reeking of shit; all the houses had open latrines. The pigs mucked around in the drain, grunting, squealing or fighting fiercely.

Jani Bhai's screams could be heard from his house. So he had got drunk today as well. Loud laughter rang out from Kamaluddin's house; seemed like some relatives were visiting. Osman walked past four other houses. Mumtaz Apa was weeping alone after her children had gone to bed. It was over a year since Pasha Bhai was killed in the Hindu-Muslim riots. How was she to cope with life with these little children, and carry on?

Osman stopped in front of his house and knocked. 'Coming!' shouted Sajida. She must be busy with something. Parveen, his younger sister, opened the door for him. Pulling the curtain aside, Osman went in to wash his feet and hands. The house, constructed during his grandparents' time, was congested. On one side, there was Osman and Sajida's bedroom. In the middle was a small verandah with a tiled roof and a small corridor, one end of which led to the outer door. At the other end, in the corner was an open toilet. A gunny sack hung like a curtain at its entrance. Next to it was a small bathroom with a shahbad stone floor, enclosed by old sarees and bedsheets for its walls. In the verandah lay a small cot, an old sewing machine in a corner, and a wooden table with beddings on it.

Wiping his hands and feet, Osman came and stood in the verandah. Sajida spread the mat and the dastarkhan, and brought the rice pot. Parveen brought the water jug and the glass. Serving himself some rice, Osman asked, 'Has everyone eaten?'

His youngest sister Nasreen replied, 'Just now, bhaiya.' She sat on a small mat near the wall, embroidering shiny beads onto a saree.

Saida Begum, who was resting on the small narrow cot alongside the mat where Osman ate his dinner, got up to make herself a paan and asked, 'Why so late today, beta?' She had been waiting for Osman for quite some time now.

Sajida joined Osman and served herself some rice.

'Zameer Bhai and his friend had come over. We were chatting.'

Saida Begum suddenly remembered and asked, 'Sajida, did you give him the omelette that we saved from lunch?'

'No, it is in the utti hanging from the roof,' said Nasreen.

Parveen brought it and served it to her brother. For a while no one spoke. Saida Begum got up and slowly walked towards the drain running along the outer wall of the lane to spit out the betel leaf juice. She walked back, sat down on her cot and said, 'Beta, those people from Annaram sent word that they would like to come and see Parveen.'

The entire household waited for Osman's response. Parveen, who had gone into the kitchen, hid there and pressed her ears against the wall. Nasreen listened while pretending to concentrate on her embroidery. Sajida bent her head down to eat.

Osman finished his dinner in silence, immersed in his own thoughts, and went out to wash his hands. He came back, drank water from the jug, wiped his hands on the towel and said, 'Not now, Ammi. We don't have a single paisa in hand. Even if we cut down on the dowry and other gifts, we need a minimum of one lakh. Where will we get the money from? We will be forced to borrow again. We still haven't repaid the loan we took for the older one, or the one we took when father fell ill. What I earn is not even enough to pay the interest on these loans. We won't be able to manage the wedding right now. We will have to borrow for everything. In any case, who will give us a loan now? Parveen's wedding has been delayed anyway. A few more days won't make a difference.'

Turning to face Saida Begum, Osman said, 'Ammi, I have been thinking of going to Dubai for a long time. Today, Kamaluddin had come with Zameer Bhai and he told me that there is an opportunity. He promised to introduce me to someone. I have a feeling that this time, my trip to Dubai will surely work out. Once I am there, we won't need to worry about anything.'

Saida Begum thought about it and said, 'You will need money to go to Dubai, too. Where are you going to get that?'

'It will cost sixty to seventy thousand. But I will manage that somehow. This time I am determined to go, even if I have to mortgage the house. I will work day and night in Dubai and get Parveen married. Ammi, if we could just wait another year ...' Osman spoke very persuasively.

'Beta, I am not sure. I am really worried. How you will manage all this?' Saida Begum reached for her paan box to make herself another paan. Sajida cleared the dishes, rolled up the mat and kept it in the corner. Parveen did not come out of the kitchen. Nasreen picked up the broom to sweep the floor clean so she could spread the beddings.

'Ammi, don't worry! I will take care of everything. You don't worry. Don't you always tell me that whatever has to happen will happen anyway? You go and rest now.' Osman got up and went into the bedroom.

Sajida went to clear up things in the kitchen. Parveen began to spread out the mattresses for the night. Saida Begum lay down on her bed, chewing her paan pensively as she tried to pick out the lice in her hair. As Parveen finished making the beds, Nasreen brought Shehnaz, Osman's eldest daughter who had fallen asleep, and put her on the bed. Then she picked up her saree, the box of shiny beads and threads, and sat down to work again. Drawing the curtains together, Parveen bolted the front door and dragged a large stone slab across for extra security. She switched off the light outside, lay down next to Nasreen and turned on the other side.

Nasreen asked Parveen, 'You have already cut the cloth. Don't you want to finish stitching Vasant auntie's blouse before sleeping?'

Parveen replied, slightly irritated, 'I will do it tomorrow.' Her mind was crowded with worries. She was already twenty-four. Must she wait another whole year? All the young women of her age were already married and had two or three children each. She felt awkward meeting them. Being unmarried makes one so restless. One wants to do something in desperation. Anything at all. That man who lived in the last house of the lane—didn't he speak to her with his eyes glued to her body every time she went to fetch water simply because she was still unmarried! She had turned away from him in anger then. But now she cannot resist the urge to look at him when he passes by.

Sajida switched off the light in the kitchen and bolted the door. Entering their bedroom, she closed the door, shifted their little son to one side and lay down next to Osman. Osman, lost in his thoughts till then, turned towards her.

'I am anxious about your going to Dubai. How will we manage here without you for so long? Won't the children miss you?'

'What to do! You will have to manage somehow ... just for five years. Then we'll be rid of all these worries for good. We can all live in peace then. Right now I have no sleep and no peace.'

Sajida put her arm around Osman and fell asleep. With his head full of thoughts, Osman could not. Work at the watch shop took up his whole day. He was forced to sell things for ten rupees or less and repair clocks and watches until his eyes watered in order to keep the few customers who came by. Yet, there was no end to his worries. Money was never enough. Whatever he earned was barely enough to manage the household. How would he repay the loans? How would he get his two sisters married? There were two growing children to think of, besides. And now Sajida is pregnant again! His sisters, his mother, no one seemed happy or content. Every day he left home early and returned only after the children had gone to sleep. There was no time or money for any leisure or entertainment. He could not indulge the children in any way. Sometimes, there wasn't even small change in his pocket. How to cope with the children's education, their books, their clothes? In the midst of all these worries, now his brother-in-law was pestering him for financial support. And caught between the two, his sister was under great stress. Osman didn't know where to turn. His life seemed completely rudderless.

Osman turned on his right side in an effort to sleep. No, it didn't look like he could sleep tonight. His mind was full of Parveen moving about the house silently. How many times had Parveen dressed up as a bride to be paraded before prospective grooms and their families? When would she really become a bride? The image of her the last time she had dressed up still lingered before his eyes. That day was full of activity. Many arrangements were made. A beautifully adorned Parveen was shown to the marriage party and then taken inside by their neighbour who had come to help. The boy's side liked the girl and seemed happy. But when they produced the dahej-farez, the list of dowry and other demands that were to be met for the wedding to take place, Osman felt faint just looking at it. Five tolas of gold, twenty tolas of silver, fifty thousand in cash, one Hero Honda motorbike, a steel almirah, colour television, Titan wristwatch, table fan, bed and mattress, a dining table with four chairs, costly cooking dishes ... the list went on and on and even included a mirror and a comb! They could give all the small items. But Osman wasn't sure how to manage the expensive things on the list. The boy's father noticed his hesitation and said, 'It is all right. Take some more time and let us know.' However, Osman decided it was best to be straight with them.

'We cannot afford all this. I had already told Asghar Khalu that we cannot give more than the jode ki rakham and a reasonable dowry. I don't know what he told you. I am sorry that you took the trouble of coming all the way. Please pardon us.'

The boy's sister protested, 'Bhai, don't say that. We can reduce the list if necessary. Please tell us what you can give. One gives what one can. Why should you apologise? Look, we all liked the girl. We have looked around a lot. People have promised good dowry. But we did not accept because we did not like the girl. These days there is a craze for grooms with a sarkari job. You would know this, of course. Just tell us how much you can give as dowry. If it is fine with us, we will settle the matter here and now.'

For a while, there was complete silence. Then the neighbourhood khala blurted out, 'These days, even those with an attendant's job are demanding lakhs in dowry. How can poor families with many daughters give so much? You should think of this before asking. This family has not yet come out of the debts incurred during the first girl's wedding. What can the poor brother possibly say now? He carries the burden of the entire household upon his shoulders.'

'What is the point in saying all these things? Can a girl hope to get married these days without a lakh at least? We also got our girl married with a dowry of one lakh,' a female relative from the groom's side said sharply.

Osman intervened to cut short this heated exchange and said, 'I will let you know in a few days.' With that, all further discussion was halted. While leaving, the groom's side took an assurance from Osman that he would inform them of his decision soon. Before she left, the groom's sister came to the room where Parveen sat, head covered and bent. She lifted Parveen's face gently with her forefinger, caressed her cheek, kissed Parveen's hand and left.

As soon as they left, Saida Begum anxiously said, 'Beta, you could have quoted some figure at least. Why didn't you?'

Parveen came out of the room and stood there, eager to hear her brother's reply.

'Ammi, we know this from experience, we cannot possibly reduce the figure they quoted to half, can we? Even that half amounts to seventy or eighty thousand. And the dawat will cost us nearly thirty thousand. We can't afford so much, Ammi. This rishta is not for us.' Osman's voice trembled as he spoke. It broke his heart to see the tears in Parveen's eyes. But what could he do! No one said a word. Parveen went inside. Osman turned to Sajida to signal that she should go and console Parveen.

Nasreen was clearing the jugs, glasses of water, tea cups, and the kishti containing aromatic spices like cardamom, fennel seeds and betel nuts, besides the surma and fragrant itr, so that she could remove the carpet and the cushions. Saida Begum sat on her cot, making her paan and muttering to herself, 'Everyone is asking for dowry in lakhs. Fifty or sixty thousand seems nowhere enough to get a girl married. How will our girls ever get married? When will we see an end to all our troubles?'

The neighbourhood khala got up from the stool and declared, 'What is the point of getting worried, behen? Who knows where one shall find one's kismat ka joda and who is one's destined partner! As they say, Allah ke darbar mein der hai, andher nahin. There may be delays in Allah's court, but never darkness. Marriages will happen, if not today, then tomorrow. Don't you worry, especially when you have a son like Osman; he is considerate and thoughtful.' Saying this, she left.

As he mulled over these memories, it became another sleepless night for Osman. There were so many such nights now in his thirty-year life.

The next day onwards, Osman got busy with tasks related to his Dubai trip. His passport was ready, so that was one expense less. The man whom Kamaluddin had introduced him to had said that the entire trip would cost sixty thousand. By a quirk of fate, someone bought the watch shop. It fetched twenty-four thousand for Osman—fourteen thousand for the merchandise, and ten thousand in lieu of a rent advance. Sajida's gold was roughly one tola and fetched four thousand. Zameer Bhai gave him a loan of ten thousand with interest. The house fetched another fifteen thousand when mortgaged. A close relative loaned five thousand on condition that Osman would inform him of employment opportunities in Dubai. Osman did a round of all his friends and relatives, borrowing a five hundred here and a thousand there, to gather the sixty thousand required for the Dubai trip. His heart trembled with fear at the thought of the innumerable debts he was piling up.

The night before his departure to Dubai, a gulposhi ceremony was organised. Osman's sister Nusrat, her husband and their two children came home. Close relatives and the neighbourhood aunt joined in. Osman was adorned with shiny floral garlands. Osman and Sajida were seated side by side with their son Kaleem in the middle. Osman had tied a kerchief on his head and Sajida had covered her head with her saree pallu. The house was full of people. The men sat on stools and on the cot. Women stood by the side. Children surrounded Osman and Sajida. The first one to greet them was Nusrat. She had prepared a kishti, a platter of garlands, sandalwood powder, a quarter kilo of sweets, all covered with a shiny cloth. She kept it before the couple. She took out the sandal bowl, applied the sandal paste on Osman's neck with three fingers, on both sides of his adam's apple, on his chest and back. She did the same with her sister-in-law. She was about to apply it to Kaleem when an older woman said, 'Apply the paste well'. Nusrat followed the advice with affection. She garlanded her brother and tied small floral strings on his wrist. She fed him some of the mysorepak from the sweet box. She took a laddoo in hand to feed her sister-in-law. Sajida opened her mouth. Nusrat teased her, 'Wider, open wider!' There was laughter and someone cracked a joke. Sajida's face widened with a big smile. Nusrat promptly pushed a full laddoo into her mouth. People took sides and began to tease either Sajida or Nusrat. After feeding a sweet to Kaleem, Nusrat circled her hand around the three of them, pressed her knuckles to her temples and cracked them loudly to ward off the evil eye. An old woman commented, 'Oh, hear them crack! Just shows how much she loves her brother and sister-in-law!' Nusrat stepped aside, carrying her kishti covered with the shining cloth. The others followed a similar routine. Some people's knuckles made a loud noise while others' didn't. The running commentary about knuckle-cracking made the evening merry.

Towards the end, Parveen and Nasreen also gifted flower garlands to the couple, bought from money they had been saving for a long time. 'Now stand up,' someone instructed the couple. Some suggested that the two should greet the brother-in-law first and others insisted that they greet Saida Begum. Osman and Sajida got up from their seats, looking beautiful adorned with garlands around their necks. Sajida bent down to touch Osman's feet, greeting him with, 'As-salam-alaikum'. Responding to the greeting of the women present with 'Walaikum salam,' Osman saluted all the older women, his brother-in-law, and then moved towards Saida Begum and bent down to touch her feet.

Lifting Osman by his shoulders, Saida Begum blessed him, 'Live a hundred years, beta, live till your teeth fall off. May Allah keep you safe, give you good earnings ...' And saying so, she broke down. 'How will I live without you for so long, my son! How will you live so far away from all of us? It is your burdens and responsibilities that are compelling you to leave this land.' Osman, too, could not restrain his tears as he embraced her. He had never stayed away from his mother for more than ten days at a time. Suddenly, the house began to reverberate with wails. Sajida, Parveen and Nasreen, who had somehow controlled themselves until then, also began to sob, holding on to Osman and Saida Begum. Seeing the elders, the children joined the chorus of crying, unable to understand what was happening. Despite repeated assurances from relatives, the family was inconsolable. The entire scene brought tears to the eyes of the neighbours and other onlookers.

On the second day, Osman left for his voyage. Before leaving, he first went into his room. He hugged Sajida and kissed her as she wrapped herself around him and wept. He consoled her, wiped the tears from her face and told her to take care of the children and his mother. He hoped she would be able to cope with any difficulties that may arise in his absence. Drawing his children closer, Osman kissed them, taking care not to shed the tears clouding his eyes. He hurriedly brushed the tears away. But who could clear the growing mist of pain in his heart! Then he went to Saida Begum to pay his respects. The old mother gathered her courage and blessed him again. She also took a vow to take Osman to the Janapad Saidulu Dargah and offer a sacrifice on his first trip back from Dubai. Bidding his sisters farewell, Osman assured them that he would call them coming Friday on Salim Bhai's number. Salim lived in the adjoining street. The entire family accompanied him till the end of the street. Turning the street corner, he waved his hand with a heavy heart to say a last goodbye as many hands returned the farewell, and he disappeared from sight. Tears welled up in everyone's eyes. The house wept the whole night, unable to come to terms with Osman's absence.

It was Jumma that day. Right from dawn, there was furious activity in the household. After the morning meal, Sajida and Parveen cleared up the house and polished the floor with a fresh coat of dung. The entire family bathed by turns and dressed in clean clothes. Sajida bathed the children first and took out clean clothes for them from the box, kurta-pyjama and a cap for Kaleem, and shirt-shalwar with a headscarf for Shehnaz. Once dressed, she sent them off to the mosque in the adjoining street for the Friday prayers. The women offered namaz at home, taking a little longer than usual. At last, when it was four in the evening, the entire family went to Salim Bhai's house to wait for the phone call from Dubai. Salim Bhai had gone out, but his wife Shahina was around and they chatted with her and her two daughters, Safiya and Asiya, and time passed by.

As dusk settled and the evening grew darker, the family's anxiety increased. Sajida's children grew restive and irritable. Saida Begum, Parveen and Nasreen tried their best to distract and humour them. Safiya and Asiya went in to finish their household chores. Shahina made small talk. Sajida and the others listened to her chit-chat half-heartedly, their ears on the phone. The children were running in and out of the house. At six o' clock, Saida Begum said, 'Osman said he would call. Why hasn't he called till now?' Sajida said, 'I hope all is well with him. I fear something is not right'. Parveen said, 'Who knows if he has access to a phone there? Maybe he is just preoccupied with work.' But the anxiety and fear slowly crept into their hearts.

Meanwhile, to pass the time, Shahina Bhabhi started recounting tales of all the troubles that migrants to Dubai encountered there. Till then, her chatter had not reached their ears. But now her tales of Arabistan began to rake up fear in their hearts.

'So, my relative Jameer was a truck driver here. He went to Arabistan on a driver's visa. They asked him to drive a trawler. Their vehicles are huge, much bigger than the ones here. He got a little jittery. That's it, he was asked to tend sheep instead! He didn't see another human being for days. Hungry and thirsty, he begged them to let him return to India. After a lot of difficulty, he was sent home. Poor man! He now drives a lorry and pays the interest on the hefty loan that he took to go to Arabistan.

'You see people believe that all their problems will be solved once they go there. But who knows what troubles they will face there? Many people go as maids. Since it is a matter of shame to work as a maid servant, they will declare that they have got a decent job there. I believe some are even engaged in cleaning toilets. I have heard that the people there are very arrogant. Khala, I heard that one is not supposed to question them at all. Even a small mistake can prove to be very costly!'

Safiya brought tea for everyone and as she handed them their cups, she added her bit to her mother's running commentary. 'In the film *Naam*, the hero pesters his friend to send him to Dubai. Once he reaches there, he gets caught in a smuggling case. And Allah! What troubles he endures! In the end, he tearfully begs his friend to take him back to India. The friend tries his utmost. But the police shoot down the hero in the end,' she summed up the film.

'In my grandmother's village there was this man who took huge loans to go abroad. An agent kept him in a hotel in Mumbai on the pretext that the flight was scheduled for the next day. He took his money and went out, and he never came back. This man searched for the agent everywhere, and then realised he had been duped. Unable to face the prospect of returning to his village, he hanged himself in the hotel room. Poor fellow!

'Why, didn't you see the report in the newspaper the other day? A man went to Dubai and was jailed. His family searched for him everywhere they could, but gave up hope in the end. He returned home after seven years, I believe. He said there were so many like him locked up in Dubai jails. People who get duped try to stealthily cross over to the neighbouring country, but they get caught and are jailed.'

Saida Begum and Sajida grew more and more anxious and uneasy as they listened to these horrifying tales. Did Osman also suffer a similar fate, they wondered.

Just then the phone rang. Their hopes rose. But it was not Osman. Shahina spoke to someone else. It had grown quite dark by then. Sajida left to cook the evening meal at home. After a while, Parveen and Nasreen also left, carrying the sleepy children in their arms. Saida Begum kept sitting there, waiting for her son's call. Parveen returned after a while to call her. 'Ammi, let us go now. It is late. They must be ready to go to bed.' Before leaving, they requested Shahina to inform them just in case the phone call came.

At home, no one was in the mood to talk, or eat. Saida Begum chewed her paan and lay down in bed, pensively scratching her head with a finger. That night, neither the mother nor the wife could sleep. Several nights passed. Saida Begum grew weak and could not get up from bed. The unmarried sisters grew sick with the worry of advancing age. Sajida gave birth to another daughter. Days turned into weeks, and months, and years. After three years, the man who had given a loan on the house occupied it as the mortgage on the house could not be redeemed. Hapless and stricken with shame, the women moved into a rented house. Their attempts to search for Osman proved futile. They gradually withdrew from life. When the women were drowned in sorrow, who was there to console the bewildered children? Carrying an image of Osman in their sunken eyes, devoid of hope, his family continued to wait for him. With their faces turned towards Qibla, they continued to pray for his safe return.

Translated by **Rama S. Melkote**

12

Urs

As soon as I reached Imliban bus station, I rushed to buy a ticket to Nalgonda town, and proceeded to occupy my seat in the bus. As the bus moved out of the city of Hyderabad, my thoughts, too, moved along with it. It was getting late. My sisters must be annoyed. 'You told us to be at the hillock by eight. Why are you so late?' they will say.

Whenever I visit Nalgonda or even picture it in my head, it is those two hillocks that first come to mind. For some strange reason, the entire town is located around and between those two hillocks. One of them is known as Lateef Shah Wali Pahad, named after the Lateef Shah Wali Dargah which is located on it. Every year, an urs is celebrated on the hillock and a noisy and festive fair takes place at the foot of the hill. For children it is carnival time; for adults climbing the hillock during the urs offers a pleasant break from normal routine.

The thought of urs brought Ruksana to my mind. Her image filled my eyes and overflowed with my tears as guilt rose up in my throat to choke me. The bus briefly stopped at Dilsukhnagar bus station before proceeding.

As a child how eagerly I would look forward to the urs! Three days ahead of the festival, the steps cut into the hillock would be freshly whitewashed, looking as if they led straight to the clouds. When they were lit up at night, they were as seductive as a long flower-bedecked braid. I would wait for Friday, my heart bursting with excitement and the desire to mingle with the crowds, merge with its boisterous laughter, fly like a kite over the hillock.

On Thursday evening, everyone got dressed in their best clothes and reached the hillock. It was the day of the 'sandal' when Lateef Saab was decorated with sandalwood paste and shroud. The foot of the hillock would soon be milling with people. Women rested in the shade while men took the children to the fair to buy them sweetmeats. Older children wandered around with their own friends. There were so many different kinds of toys and shiny things. For those who had crossed that toy-crazy age, there were spectacles, pens, belts, caps and other decorative items. For girls, there were lots of beautiful things. After the children's toys, it was earrings, nose rings, necklaces, finger rings, kajal, surma boxes, bangles, slippers, clothes and burqas that dominated the fair. It was a rich, vibrant and magical world. Amongst all those bright multi-coloured balloons, each of us was transformed into a different hue and we floated around the fair, wide-eyed with wonder.

The 'sandal' procession started from the Jam Majeed area. As it slowly reached the hillock, the entire area got flooded with people. Despite the police barricade, some people still managed to enter the path of the procession. Men wearing white clothes occupied the front row. Women in black burqas stood behind them in rows. Children mostly stayed in the arms of the adults. By the time the procession reached the first archway or kamaan on its way up the hillock, the crowd turned into a tidal wave. The procession found it difficult to move beyond the first step. Everyone was eager to touch the 'sandal' with their hands and forehead, and do the same for their children. It was sheer magic that had to be experienced to be believed.

The bus stopped at Hayathnagar bus station. A few passengers without ticket alighted to buy them. I informed the driver and went to have a cup of tea. After I returned, the bus moved again.

Whenever I think of urs, I am reminded of black burqas. Perhaps because I ran after them in the early days of my youth! In the urs of my second year of graduation, I came face to face with those eyes—moon-like amid dark clouds, big, beautiful kohled eyes on a fair face ... those white eyes with dark pupils at their centre, they were incredibly attractive. I never knew if they followed me or if I followed them. Several times during the urs, we ran into each other. Our eyes met, and it felt as if we had known each other for a long time.

That was how it began. For all the ten days of the urs, I would cycle to the hillock and roam around the alleys of the fair. I would search each shop intently as if I wanted to buy something. But of course I wasn't looking for anything. I was only hoping to catch a glimpse of her, to savour the look in those warm eyes and to glide on their laughter. On the last day when the shops were about to close, I somehow managed to ask her what her name was. 'Ruksana,' she replied, and asked for mine. 'Yousuf,' I said. When I asked her what she studied, she said, 'Intermediate, second year'. Her friends began to tease her and giggle. I found out which college she went to. In the end I pleaded with her, 'Why don't you remove your naqab so I can see your face?' She simply said, 'We will meet again here tomorrow evening,' and left.

I couldn't sleep that night. If my heart was beating so rapidly, I wondered what state she might be in. I waited impatiently for daybreak, and for the day to pave the way for the evening. She came to the hillock with a friend whom she had persuaded to accompany her. The place we had planned to meet was a little above the shops, next to the steps on the hillock. She was sitting behind a huge rock. Following them, I reached the spot and sat down next to her. 'Why don't you remove your naqab now?' I asked her. She untied the knot underneath her chin and removed the naqab. Her face shone like the full moon on a dark night. I could not help saying, Wah! 'So how do I look?' she asked with a smile. 'As if the moon has left the sky and reappeared here, next to me,' I replied. I was showered with that moonlit laughter again. We chatted for half an hour, measuring time with the speed and sound of our heartbeats.

From that day on, we met every day at someplace or the other. Neither of us was at peace on the days we couldn't meet. At the end of that year, Ruksana told me with tears in her eyes that her family wanted to discontinue her education once she completed the Intermediate. She was inconsolable. I did not know what to do. I couldn't show her a way out nor could I reassure her. I had three younger sisters. Only one was married by then. I was yet to complete my own studies. What could I do?

'Will you marry me?' she asked me straight.

My heart shrivelled up in agony. On what strength, on what basis could I say yes? My household was in shambles. If I got married, it would deteriorate further. How could I say yes?

'Can't you stall your marriage for two or three years?' I asked.

'No, my family wants me to get married to my cousin this summer. My aunt and he are both in a hurry.'

'What does he do for a living?'

'He is a mechanic.'

'A mechanic?! Why does he want to marry a girl who is more educated than him? What is your family thinking? Won't they even consider for a minute what it would do to you?'

'That is the desperate state my parents are in.'

'Then why did they educate you?'

'I fought with them and managed to study till now.'

'You should fight now, too! Tell them that you won't marry him.'

'They are not listening to me anymore.'

'What will you do now?'

'You tell me!'

I tried to explain, 'I cannot marry you right now, Ruksana. I have two unmarried sisters at home. My family is not in a good shape.'

'Then why did you love me? Didn't you think of all this before?'

I was speechless. Ruksana left the place in tears. I followed her on my cycle. I could see that she was weeping inside the burqa. I pleaded with her not to. My cycle came to a stop once we reached her street. She moved on ahead. Just before she entered her house, she turned back once to look at me. I never imagined that it would be my last glimpse of her.

After this, I made innumerable rounds of her house. Ruksana was nowhere to be seen. I would ring my cycle bell, which I had fixed for her sake. Earlier she would have rushed out as soon as she heard the tring-tring of the bell. Now, she did not. I almost went crazy for a few days. I was unable to eat or sleep. When I slept on the cot outside, I saw only her face in the moon. I wept inconsolably. If at all I slept, I would dream of her through the night. Seeing my forlorn and distracted state, my family grew quite concerned.

At the end of that summer, Ruksana's house was brightly lit up for wedding festivities. I wept till I thought my heart would burst. Ruksana got married. Like a crow that had lost its chicks, I kept hovering around her house. But of what use was it now.

As soon as the bus stopped near the big clock in Nalgonda town, I quickly alighted and started walking towards the hillock. On the road leading to the hillock, a big welcome signboard had been erected. 'Lateef Shah Wali Dargah' it announced in Urdu, Telugu and English. After the first archway, push-carts and shops appeared. I crossed them and walked on further. One look at the hillock stirred up a rush of memories of childhood joy. A lot of trees have been planted since then. The place was teeming with people. I walked towards the neem trees on the right side. My three sisters were standing there. Their faces lit up with smiles as soon as they spotted me, but they were just as quick to express their annoyance at my delay. Greeting them, I took a good look at all of them. In no time, my sisters' children were all over me. Enquiring after every member of the family, by the time I herded them all—my three sisters, their children, one younger brother and his wife—onto the hillock, it was eight thirty. I tried to catch up with news from our village as we started our climb. They began to fill me in with the latest. They had already told me on phone that mother did not want to climb the hillock and would not be joining us. I had also informed them that my wife would not be here as she was running a fever.

Since it was the first day of the urs, the steps to the dargah were filled with people. By eleven, their numbers would grow. Even now at eight thirty, quite a few people were already descending the steps after having visited the dargah. We prayed to the first step of the first kamaan and began our ascent. A fakir rattling his kashkol brushed our heads with peacock feathers, blessing us. Dropping some small change into his kashkol, I moved ahead. The fakirs touched everyone's forehead with peacock feathers. They were seated on both sides of the staircase, calling out 'Amma! Baba!' as they sought alms. Some were blind, a few were disabled, and some lepers. It pained me to see them. While climbing up, everyone, especially the children distributed small change that their parents had given them to the fakirs.

I was climbing slowly with my niece in my arms. If my childhood memory served me right, there should be fourteen hundred steps. As a child, I remembered climbing it twice in a day. I greeted several people I knew among those ascending or descending the steps.

'What did you bring to eat?' I asked my eldest sister.

'Roti and dal,' she replied.

'Oh! Is that all?' I said dejected.

Unable to contain herself, the second one blurted out, 'We also brought what you like.'

'You got the fried stuff, too?' I asked, my mouth watering.

'Yes, we bought one and a half kilos. We fried one half and made beef curry out of the other half,' she said.

We greeted relatives, neighbours and people we knew from our village as we climbed up.

'Amma! My feet are aching! Let us stop for a while,' my eldest sister pleaded after a while.

We stepped aside from the flight of stairs and sat down on the rocks. My younger brother and his wife continued their climb, engrossed in chatting. It was the first urs after their wedding. When they realised that we had halted, they came back looking for us. The sun was getting hotter. Those who were thirsty drank water and gave some to the children. From our spot on the hillock, we could clearly see all of Nalgonda that lay in front of us. A portion of the left side was also visible. The second hillock blocked the view on the right.

We resumed our ascent. As we climbed higher, the town houses looked like toy houses and the roads, like thin lines. We stopped again after a while. My brother pointed out the village road and some trees to his wife and told her that it was our village, Keshurajupally. I also tried to spot our village. I glanced around at the people climbing the hillock. There were more non-Muslims than Muslims. Here was true bahujan culture, I thought. As the dargah was a Muslim place of worship, there was no bottu marking anyone's forehead. Their identity could be gleaned only from their clothes and the language they spoke. My thoughts drifted. While Muslims were moving away from the dargah culture due to the propaganda of the jamats, non-Muslims were moving away from them due to the propaganda of the Hindutva organisations and parties. But thanks to the ever increasing population, the dargahs continued to flourish. I heard that the maulvis now preached in mosques that Muslims should not visit the dargahs and perform sijda there. This pained me. If this trend continued, what will happen to this urs?

My gaze fell upon a burqa climbing up the steps. The face looked familiar from far. A young girl was walking next to her. The woman held a small boy by the hand. As I watched, she moved up closer. My heart suddenly skipped a beat. It was Ruksana! Stunned, I stood there rooted to the spot. Ruksana moved closer.

My sister asked me, 'Shall we go?' Ruksana reached the step closest to us. She didn't glance in our direction and moved past.

'Ruksana ...' I called out almost involuntarily.

She looked around, surprised. For a moment she didn't know who had called her. Then she saw me, and was startled. I quickly recovered from my initial shock and invited her to join our group. She greeted everyone with a 'Salam alaikum' and walked towards me, holding her son's hand.

'How are you?' I asked.

'As you can see,' she murmured, removing her headscarf.

My family watched us both curiously. I introduced Ruksana to them. My sisters shook her hand, received her greetings, and threw me questioning glances. I told them that we got to know each other in the urs during our college days. They looked at me sceptically but kept their suspicions to themselves.

I watched Ruksana. She watched me as well, but she would avert her gaze whenever our eyes met. I offered her a glass of water. 'I have water with me,' she replied. I could see she was tense. I took her little son into my arms. A beautiful child! All her three children were light-skinned; the girls seemed to take after their mother. I was thrilled to meet Ruksana. Memories of our meetings and our walks and conversations around the hillock filled my mind.

My second sister started a conversation with Ruksana. 'Where do you stay?'

'Here. In Hyderguda.'

Oh, so she was given in marriage to a family in Nalgonda itself, I thought.

'Isn't their father here?' my elder sister asked, pointing to Ruksana's children.

'No, he had some work,' she replied.

'Shall we carry on?' my younger brother asked.

We moved on. Since I was carrying Ruksana's son, my younger brother had to carry our niece. I chatted with Ruksana's daughter, asking her which class she was in. She was eight. When she spoke, she sounded just like Ruksana. My brother and sister-in-law led the group, followed by my sisters' children, followed by my second sister and Ruksana. I walked behind them along with Ruksana's daughter. My youngest sister and her five-year-old son walked behind us. She wasn't very happy about Ruksana joining our group; her face showed her displeasure.

We drew closer to the top. With a little more effort, we would reach the dargah. Ruksana turned around, and was reassured to see that her son was still safely perched on my shoulders. Our eyes met for a brief moment and her face lit up with unexpected joy, before she turned back and continued her climb. 'Let's take a break here,' I said. I wanted to take a good look at the town spread out far below us. Also, it was tiring to climb carrying a child on one's shoulder.

All of us stopped to catch our breath and to watch the scenery. The hillock on the right, known as Kapurala Gutta, was almost the same height as the Lateef Saab Gutta. Between the two hillocks, the crowded lanes and houses of the Jam Majeed area were visible. We looked up. We could see the dargah and the tree next to it. Green flags tied to the branches fluttered in the breeze.

We moved on again. The dargah drew closer. Fakirs kept shouting, 'Baba! Baba!' from both sides of the steps. Distributing small change, we kept on going. At last we reached the top. Once there, I went to Ruksana to ask her to stay with us. There is a big rock on the left side of the dargah. The rock and the tree next to it look like a head with a hippy village haircut. We made place for ourselves amidst the trees behind the rock and settled down. The children wandered off to play. Once we had taken a breather, we asked my brother and his wife to stay back with the children and our things, while my sisters, Ruksana and I went into the dargah. They could go in once we returned. I tied a kerchief around my head. The women drew their saree pallus over their heads. A heady mixture of fragrances—incense, jasmine and rose—transported us into another world. We circled the dargah three times along with all the others. My sisters stood outside the door, got the coconuts cracked and offered fateha. Women were not allowed inside. I entered the dargah through the door meant for men.

Lateef Saab's mazar was located right in the middle of the dargah. It stood at a height and was covered with garlands and flowers. I looked up. The roof of the dargah looked beautiful from inside. The rush of people increased. I will have to move quickly now. The caretakers who offer the fateha on your behalf have long beards. I went to the left side of the grave, kneeled down, put my head on the garlands and pushed my forehead onto the flowers. It felt so soothing and peaceful to feel the cool soft petals on my face. I inhaled deeply to fill my lungs with their fragrance and remained like that for a few moments. When I got up, I found Ruksana's eyes gazing at me intently from the opposite doorway. My sisters had stepped aside after offering fateha. I returned her gaze without blinking. This time she did not look away. So many emotions, so many memories danced in those eyes. My heart grew heavy. I turned to go out. She also turned back.

Stepping out of the dargah, I glanced at the tree on the left. When I was a boy, my mother would tie flags onto the tree, wishing for various things to end our difficulties—marriage for my sisters; good results in our tenth class exams; jobs for all of us. Only she knew which of her prayers were answered. I would simply run to the hillock with the green flag in my hand whenever she asked me to. That is all I knew.

All of us returned to our spot behind the rock. My younger brother and his wife started for the dargah as soon as we returned. The children were roaming around the place. Ten steps cut into the side of the rock led down to a spring. It used to be full of sweet water in our childhood. How much ever we drank from it, it always filled up again. Later, however, it dried up. There was rumour that someone had washed their hands in it after finishing a meal. The place is full of such real and fantastical stories.

My younger sisters' children came to take sweets and coconut from their mother and disappeared soon after. Ruksana's daughter went off to play along with her younger brother. Even my sisters had wandered away. Only Ruksana and I remained sitting there.

'How are you?' I asked.

'I am fine. Did you ever remember me later on?'

'I never forgot you, Ruksana.'

'Every year, whenever I climbed up the hillock, I would always look for you. But I never saw you even once,' she said, half annoyed.

'Is that so? Even I have looked for you every time I have come here. It seems we never came at the same time. Anyway, it has been such a long time since I climbed the hillock.' I was going to ask about her husband, but stopped myself. Why should he come between us now? Instead, I asked her, 'Did you discontinue your studies then?'

She was lost in her own thoughts and didn't hear what I said. My heart writhed with the pain and guilt of having let her down.

'Why didn't you ever come to see me then?' I asked.

'My uncle saw me speaking to you once and reported it at home. You told me there was no way you could marry me right then. So what could I do? They fixed my marriage with my cousin. I tried hard to convince them that I wanted to study further. But no one listened to me.'

'But in the end it all turned out well, didn't it?' I said.

Without responding to my query, she gave me a strange look that I could not read. Then she said, 'I remembered you often,

Yousuf. In that one year, for reasons I am not sure of, I grew very fond of you. It may have been because you were educated, or my cousin was not; or it may have been due to my own liking for education. When I could not marry you, my heart dried and shrivelled up. It took me a long time to recover. Being a man, you seem to have fared quite well, unlike me.'

Before I could respond, Ruksana's children returned. The others also joined in soon after and everyone settled down. I was glad to see my sisters busily chatting with Ruksana. I took in my fill of her. Her face shone just like the full moon I remembered. There was in her face a fullness that was missing earlier. She, too, returned my gaze. There was affection and warmth in that gaze. I wondered why her husband hadn't accompanied her. Perhaps they were not so close. Many suspicions arose in my mind.

Our respective tiffin boxes were opened and we exchanged the eatables with much affection, chatting merrily over this and that as we ate our lunch. My sister's son asked me, 'What is the significance of this dargah, Mamu?'

I began to explain in detail.'All these dargahs belong to the Sufis. They worked for the spread of Islam. Their kindness and honesty, their empathy for the poor, for the oppressed malas, madigas and shudras made them like gods for these people. Dargahs were built in their memory after their death. Both Muslims and non-Muslims come here. It is sacred to both. Such mingling of Muslims and others is culturally very important.'

My second sister chipped in,'And that is why my brother makes sure that we all meet here during the urs every year!'

Conversation flowed smoothly. Soon it was time for all of us to return. This time, Ruksana and I followed my brothers and sisters. I still carried Ruksana's son on my shoulder. She inquired about me and my wife with interest. I drank in her beauty with my eyes as we walked down the hillock. Three-fourths of the way down, she took out her mobile and called someone. I hadn't taken her number. I should remember to take her number. The descent didn't take much time and before I knew it, we had already reached the foot of the hill.

We stopped near the neem trees where we had first assembled. The rush of people increased as it grew dark and the place became noisy. I felt sad because Ruksana would now leave. I asked for her phone number. She continued to talk but didn't give her number. I asked her again. She changed the topic of conversation but still didn't offer it. I felt bad.

'Does your husband look after you well?' I asked.

'He used to be quite obstinate. I suffered initially. But he has changed now. I completed my Hindi Diwan exams and I wrote my District Selection Committee exam for school teachers recently. I will definitely clear it. I want to take up a teacher's job,' she said determinedly.

Just then, her cell phone rang. 'My husband is here,' she said and grabbed the child from me. She turned to my sister and said, 'We shall meet again in the urs'. She said goodbye to all my sisters. She bade me farewell with her eyes. Eager to see her husband, my gaze followed Ruksana. I saw her husband approach her and take their son from her arms. Ruksana looked happy as she spoke to him. He looked fine. Ruksana, her husband and their three children soon merged with the crowd. The sadness of not getting her phone number lifted. Ruksana looked happy with her husband and children. That was enough for me.

I turned towards my sisters. They were busy speaking to their friends. Some of our relatives had also gathered. There was an all round festive atmosphere, people moving about in several directions at once, many conversations taking place under the trees. Perhaps it was just for this that the urs takes place—so that people can meet each other at least once every year. If I wanted to see Ruksana again, I would have to wait for the next urs. I slowly began to move out of the fair along with the others.

Translated by **A. Suneetha**

Glossary of Deccani and Telugu Terms

alai-balai (Deccani): A form of embrace popular in Telangana, especially among Muslims, where they embrace once and then embrace again, moving their heads onto the opposite shoulder the second time.

anna (Telugu): Elder brother; also used generically for an older man.

apa (Deccani): Elder sister; also used generically for an older woman.

avva or **buamma** (Telugu): Used to address elderly women, Muslims and non-Muslims alike.

babu (Telugu): A common mode of address for young men, mostly used in the Andhra region.

bagara baigan (Deccani): A Hyderabadi delicacy of gravied brinjal; bagar means tempering.

bagara rice: A delicately spiced Hyderabadi rice dish, similar to the pulao.

bahujan (Hindi): Literally meaning majority, it is a term that was used by Mahatma Jotiba Phule to refer to people involved in different forms of labour and who constitute majority of the Indian population. Phule used the term to counter the demeaning labels of 'shudra' and 'ati shudra' prevalent in Hindu society. In contemporary Indian politics, the terms 'bahujan' and 'dalit-bahujan' have become potent identities around which new political communities have been mobilised. After abolishing all discrimination based on caste, the Indian Constitution designated the castes formerly known as 'untouchable' as scheduled castes and many labouring shudra castes as backward classes, and it provided special provisions in the form of reservations to offer them protection against societal discrimination. For Skybaaba, caste contradictions and discrimination work at the level of the everyday—among relationships with friends and neighbours and in dealing with representatives of the state like the police. Some of the caste names that count as bahujan and backward class and which appear in the stories are chakali, golla and goundla.

basti (Deccani, Hindi): Derived from the term 'basna', literally to live, it is a habitation of poor, usually lower caste people in the towns of Telangana and Hyderabad. Poorly served in terms of the municipal infrastructure and state support, a basti typically consists of narrow lanes with rows of small houses packed closely together.

bayan (Deccani): The sermon given by the maulvi at the mosque before the prayers begin.

bidda (Telugu): Though the term means daughter, young people in Telangana—both men and women—are commonly addressed as bidda.

bottu (Telugu): The dot on the forehead typically worn by Hindu women.

chakali (Telugu): A washermen's caste.

chelle (Telugu): Younger sister.

chouthi (Telugu): A traditional playful ritual in which close relatives tease each other by applying colour, specifically haldi or turmeric, on each other's faces. While 'applying haldi' is widely practiced among dalits and Muslims during weddings in the Telangana region, the chouthi described by Skybaaba is particular to Nalgonda district.

dadi and **dada** (Deccani, Hindi): Paternal grandmother and grandfather.

dahej-farez, lein-dein (Deccani): Both refer to dowry and the associated exchange of wedding gifts between the families of the bride and groom.

dalcha (Telugu): A Deccani lentil soup made of Bengal gram with bottle gourd cooked in mutton fat; it is different from the regular lentil soup made from tuvar dal and bottle gourd.

damad (Deccani, Hindi): Son-in-law.

dargah (Deccani): The resting place and shrine of a locally revered pir or saint built around the mazar or grave of that saint. Popular among both Muslims and non-Muslims across castes and class, dargahs play a significant role in Skybaaba's stories. They symbolise the kind of Islam that his community has inherited, as well as their shared culture with dalit-bahujans of the region.

dastarkhan (Deccani): The colourful dining cloth spread on the floor to serve a meal. The word dastar connotes a range of meanings around food including sharing of food and the invitation to partake of food. In some districts of Telangana, the word is used by dalits to refer to the cloth used to wrap food while working in the fields.

dostana (Deccani): Friendship.

double ka meetha (Deccani): A Hyderabadi sweet dish of crisp fried bread dipped in syrup and served with saffron and cardamom flavoured condensed milk or rabri.

dua (Deccani): The prayer offered after the sermon given by the maulvi at the mosque.

fakir (Deccani): A nomadic Muslim beggar who often sings for alms outside mosques and at dargahs.

fateha (Deccani): Offerings of food, including flavoured rice, mutton curry etc. at the mazar in a dargah. Both Hindus and Muslims offer fateha.

galli (Deccani): The narrow winding lane of a basti.

golla (Telugu): A backward caste which is primarily a cattle rearing community.

goundla (Telugu): A caste group classified as backward class, generally engaged in toddy tapping.

gulposhi (Deccani): A custom of offering floral garlands on special occasions like farewells.

haat (Deccani, Hindi): A local market, typically held once a week in rural and small town areas where local produce and goods are available.

Hijri (Deccani): The Hijri year or era is the era used in the Islamic lunar calendar, beginning its count from 622 CE, the year of the flight of Prophet Muhammad and his followers from Mecca to Yathrib (later Medina), an event known as the Hijra. According to the Roman calendar, 1424 Hijri is year 2003.

ijtema, also **istema** (Deccani): A religious congregation that gathers at the local mosque for prayers or namaz, especially during Id or at someone's death; also, a global congregation of Muslims for the purpose of throwing light on the Holy Quran and its significance for achieving salvation.

jalwa (Deccani): A ceremony where the bride's face is shown to the guests assembled after the nikah is read.

jamat (Deccani): A gathering that offers the namaz collectively.

janaza (Deccani): A ritual prayer offered at funerals by the congregation to seek forgiveness for the dead person and all dead Muslims.

jode ki rakham (Deccani): The gift of money given to the bridegroom by the bride's side to buy clothes.

Jumma (Deccani): Friday, considered the most auspicious day of the week for Muslims.

jummagi (Deccani): The Friday prayer of Muslims.

kafir (Deccani): One who is not a Muslim, used chiefly by Muslims.

kakkaya (Telugu): Father's younger brother; also used in the generic sense of uncle.

kaman (Deccani): An archway.

kanjeera (Deccani): A small percussion instrument typically played by fakirs.

kashkol (Deccani): A dried pumpkin or bottle gourd shell used as a begging bowl.

khala and **khalba** (Deccani): Kinship terms for the mother's sister and her husband; khala is also used to address any older woman in the generic sense of aunt.

kishti (Deccani): Literally meaning a small boat, it is a platter of sweets, spices or betel leaves and nuts usually exchanged during matchmaking to confirm a marriage deal; it is also presented on other special occasions.

madiga (Telugu): Formerly an untouchable caste, usually assigned the task of clearing dead animal carcasses and working with leather.

mala (Telugu): Formerly an untouchable caste, malas usually work as village watchmen and local heralds.

mama/mamu and **mami** (Deccani, Hindi): Mother's brother and his wife, or maternal uncle and aunt.

marfa (Deccani): A small percussion instrument often played by fakirs.

maseri palang (Deccani): An ornately decorated bed, an essential part of the wedding gifts.

maulvi (Deccani): The one who leads the prayer in a mosque.

mazar (Deccani): The tomb of a saint locally revered by both Muslims and Hindus, around which a shrine or dargah is built.

mehr (Deccani): The ritual marriage gift by the husband to the wife in recognition of her worth, usually calculated terms of sikka, golden or silver coins. The stories however record the gradual shift from the mehr to the dowry, much like the change that came about in Hindu practices.

nani and **nana** (Deccani, Hindi): Maternal grandmother and grandfather.

naqab (Deccani): A veil that covers the face from the bridge of the nose downwards, often used by Muslim women and worn as part of the burqa; it also means mask.

niyat (Deccani): It connotes true intention guiding moral action as discussed in Islamic teachings.

panchayati (Telugu): A specific caste or community adjudication forum constituted to solve everyday disputes among its members. These are not to be confused with village panchayats, which are constitutionally created administrative bodies that are elected and normally consist of all castes and communities of people.

phuppa and **phuppi/phuppamma** (Deccani): Paternal aunt and her husband; also parents-in-law.

qabr (Deccani): Grave.

qazi (Deccani): The one who officiates a Muslim marriage or nikah as per Islamic law.

Qibla (Deccani): The direction of Kaba towards which a Muslim turns to pray by doing sijda.

ra (Telugu): A term used by close male friends while addressing each other, like 'da' in Tamil and 'abey' in Hindi. It is also used by family members while referring to a young boy in the family—'orey', 'aey ra' etc.

reddy (Telugu): A former shudra caste that became dominant due to their ownership of land and whose members have gradually brahminised/sanskritised themselves socially and culturally, which includes the practice of stigmatising dalits and bahujans.

rishta (Deccani, Hindi): The term means relationship; in the stories it refers to a marriage proposal or alliance.

rokkha (Deccani): The wedding card prepared once a match has been finalised.

sandal (Deccani): The act of applying sandalwood paste to the mazar at a dargah and a major religious practice.

shahbad (Deccani)**:** A stone used for flooring in houses and locally available in the Rangareddy district of Telangana.

sheer khorma (Deccani)**:** A sweet milk and semolina preparation, a dessert usually served both during Id and weddings.

sijda (Deccani)**:** The act of prostrating before God in the direction of the Kaba during the daily prayers.

tayaba (Deccani)**:** Father's elder brother; uncle.

thatha (Telugu)**:** Grandfather; also used generically for any old man.

Turka (Telugu)**:** A term, often derogatory, used to describe Muslims by referring to their putative origin in Turkey.

urs (Deccani)**:** The annual procession of a patron saint or pir associated with a particular dargah.

utti (Telugu)**:** A jute or coir frame that holds food containers and is hung from the rafters of a tiled or thatched roof. Many rural and mofussil houses in Telangana still use these.

voni (Telugu)**:** A long piece of fabric draped around the waist and over one shoulder by young women over a long skirt and blouse. Often referred to as the half-sari, this is different from the chunni or dupatta, which is a long stretch of fabric draped over the shoulders and worn along with a salwar-kameez or churidar-kurta.

walima (Deccani)**:** The wedding dinner hosted by the groom's family when the bride and groom's family visit each other on the first jummagi or Friday prayers after the wedding.

zohar and **magrib namaz** (Deccani)**:** The prayers of mid-afternoon and the prayers immediately after sunset respectively.

Note on Author

Shaik Yousuf Baba, who writes under the name Skybaaba, was born in Keshurajupally, five kilometres from Nalgonda town of Telangana. 'I am not sure of the exact date or year of my birth. It was around 1971 or 1972,' he says. He studied till class sixth in his village and from class seventh to B.A., in Nalgonda. He then trained as a 'drawing teacher'. His mother was Haji Begum and father, Gulam Mohammad, a police constable. The family suffered from heavy indebtedness. To tide over financial difficulties, Skybaaba first entered into a cloth trade that involved collecting money from customers in installments. Several factors led to his dropping out of college, he says—mounting debts, falling in love, and the realisation that a degree was only a means to find a job. Subsequently, he tried out a series of petty businesses—he set up a cycle-rental, sold soda and coconuts, opened a book-renting shop, a pan shop, became a 'Peerless' insurance agent and even ran a 'chitfund'! He incurred heavy losses and mounting debts forced him to go underground for a while. 'I starved. It was in this period that I met Shajahana. She accepted me as a partner with great courage despite my unemployment. We then moved to Hyderabad. After a great deal of difficulty, I became a journalist', he recounts. He worked in several newspapers thereafter and was in-charge of the literary page in a leading Telugu daily *Andhra Jyothi* until recently. Currently, he is a freelance writer, journalist and the editor of *Chaman*, a magazine on the social lives of Muslims.

Though initially interested in writing short stories, due to his involvement with the Nilagiri Sahiti Forum, under the mentorship of Dr. Sunkireddi Narayanareddi, Skybaaba began to write Muslimvada poetry. As a general secretary of the group, Skybaaba organised several meetings and discussions. After eleven years of this work, he put together the anthology of Muslim poetry, *Jagne Ki Raat* (2005) which gave rise to much debate and discussion in the Telugu literary sphere. These discussions were put together in the book *Gawai* (2006). Along with Shajahana, he also published the smallest book of poetry in Telugu called *Chand Tara* (2009). He has been centrally involved in bringing out several little magazines, some of which were short-lived such as *Telugu Dalit Voice* (2005–2006), *Mulki* (2002–2004), *Chaman* (2006–2007) and *Singidi* (2010–2011). He also brought out several books through a publishing house, Nasal Kitab Ghar. Skybaaba founded Haryali, a Muslim writers' forum, Marfa (2003–2004), a forum working for reservations for Muslims in erstwhile Andhra Pradesh, and he works as the convenor of Singidi (2010), a Telangana writers' forum of which he is a founder member. Having been active in the Telangana movement, he has put together three anthologies of poetry: *Jago-Jagao* (2009), *Quit Telangana* (2010), *Dimmisa* (2011), and *Razmiya* (2012), besides several collections of short stories: *Zakhmi Awaz* (2012), *Ek Kahani Ke Teen Rang: Cellphone Stories* (2013), *Alaayibalaayi: Stories of Bahujans* (2015) and *Bechare: Bhagna Prema Kadhalu* (2015). He has co-edited anthologies of *Telangana Katha* 2014 and 2015. His first novel *Aapa* and a collection of literary essays, *Jagao*, appeared in 2015. He strongly believes there is a need for social movement among contemporary Muslims. The writers he admires most are Maupassant, Basheer and Manto. Skybaaba can be reached at skybaaba@gmail.com

Notes on Translators

R. Akhileshwari is an award-winning journalist who spent thirty-five years writing about people's issues, especially about women, children, poverty and environment in Telugu, Urdu and English. She has also been a university teacher, researcher and a television producer.

Uma Maheswari Bhrugubanda teaches in the Department of Cultural Studies, English and Foreign Languages University, Hyderabad. She is also a member of Anveshi Research Centre for Women's Studies (hereafter Anveshi). A doctorate in anthropology from Columbia University, she is currently working on a book on Telugu cinema. Her research interests are Telugu literature and cinema, religion and secularism, cinema studies and feminist theory. She has been translating contemporary Telugu fiction into English and is keen on tracking the changing contours and socio-political role of literature in Telugu. She is also interested in critically evaluating the activity of translation and production of knowledge.

Christopher Chekuri teaches South Asian history at San Francisco State University. He is interested in pre-colonial histories of the Deccan as a crossroads between religions, economies, and empires.

Kiranmayi Indraganti has a PhD in film studies and is working on a book based on her doctoral research. She is a documentary film maker who has made over 10 documentaries. Her published work includes a book of English translations of the Romantic poet,

Devulapalli Krishna Sastry. Over the last decade her translations of Telugu writers such as Sikhamani, Ghantasala Nirmala, Kondepudi Nirmala, Vimala, Endluri Sudhakar, Heccharke, Indraganti Janaki Bala and others have featured in collections of contemporary Indian poetry and fiction including *Indian Literature*.

Rama S. Melkote is a founder member of Anveshi and retired as professor of political science from Osmania University, Hyderabad. Author of several works on international politics, she was also part of the editorial team that produced the book, *We Were Making History: Women and the Telangana Uprising* (1989) and its Telugu version, *Manaku Teliyani Mana Charitra: Telangana Raitanga Poratam lo Streelu* (1986). She was one of the editors of the volume *French Feminism: An Indian Anthology* (2003), and the co-editor of *Streevada Rajakeeyalu: Varthamana Charchalu* (2008), a collection of Telugu translations of Indian feminist writings from English. For the last three decades, Rama has been active in the women's movement, campaigns for workers' rights, human rights, and the right to food.

A. Suneetha is a Senior Fellow and Coordinator of Anveshi. A doctorate in political science, her research interests include feminist theory and politics of family, secularism and feminist politics, Muslim women's activism and Muslim politics in Hyderabad. Her articles have appeared in the *Economic and Political Weekly* and the *Indian Journal of Gender Studies*. She regards translation as a political obligation, especially for bilingual intellectuals located in vernacular public spheres. She is also part of the editorial team of the bilingual quarterly *Anveshi Broadsheet on Contemporary Politics*.

D. Vasanta is a longstanding member of Anveshi, and Professor Emeritus at the Department of Linguistics, Osmania University, Hyderabad. She has been an active researcher in the fields of language, linguistics and education, especially school education and education for children with disabilities. She was part of the editorial team of the Anveshi Different Tales project which produced alternative children's stories in Telugu, Malayalam and English. She is also a senior translator with several translations to her credit, notably, translation of the English feminist novel *The Yellow Wallpaper* (2001) and the graphic book on Dr. B. R. Ambedkar, *Bhimayana* (2012), into Telugu.